A

I'm Just Saying...

a collection of essays
by Sarah Smiley

Ballinger Publishing
41 N. Jefferson Street, Suite 402
Pensacola, FL 32502
www.ballingerpublishing.com

I'm Just Saying...

Printed in the United States of America

Set in Revival

First Printing: August 2008

ISBN-13 **978-0-9791103-1-3**
ISBN-10 **0-9791103-1-9**

Sarah Smiley
www.SarahSmiley.com

Ballinger Publishing
41 N. Jefferson Street, Suite 402
Pensacola, FL 32502
www.ballingerpublishing.com

Editor: Kelly Oden
Cover design: Megan Youngblood
Book design: Rita Laymon and Kelly Oden
Copyeditors: Megan Youngblood and Austin Holt
Sarah Smiley headshot courtesy of Rae Leytham Photography

Praise For Sarah's Columns and *I'm Just Saying ...*

" ... funny and always humane ... an unexpected voice ... "
The New York Times

"A witty observer of her life and times!"
The Times-Record, Brunswick, Maine

"It is that wry take on the life of a military spouse ... one that questions the rules and regulations of the shadow military she embodies, that Smiley does best."
The New York Times

"Sarah Smiley's columns are funny, smart and real. If military-spouse humor writers had ranks, she would be, at minimum, a general."
Dave Barry, author

"Sarah Smiley's columns read like amusing dispatches from your favorite friend, rather than two-dimensional words on a page. Smiley has the knack of turning the ordinary and not-so-ordinary travails of a modern-day military wife into an absorbing narrative. There's nothing stoic about this Navy wife who writes with the kind of three-beer honesty that seems both amusing and brave at the same time."
Frank Cerabino, columnist, *The Palm Beach Post*

"Witty, whimsical and wise, [*I'm Just Saying...*] will put a grin on your face."
Tim Bete, Director of the Erma Bombeck Writers' Workshop,
author of *Guide To Pirate Parenting*

"Sarah Smiley captures military family life like no other—with endearing and descriptive writing that brings both laughs and tears."
The Bradenton Herald

"In Sarah Smiley's wonderfully wacky world, Santa speaks Pig Latin, fat clothes are never discarded, and Amish Friendship bread becomes frightfully unfriendly. *I'm Just Saying ...* hilariously documents the misadventures of a military family. Each column is a carefully polished gem."
Karin Gillespie, author of *Dollar Daze*

"Insightful. Patriotic. Guaranteed to tickle your funny bone. This delightful read will remind you of the universal (and hilarious) lessons of motherhood and give you a renewed appreciation for military families. With insight and humor, Sarah Smiley helps us understand the sacrifices of military families and reminds us how essential it is to be able to laugh at ourselves. This collection of stories shares the myriad of blessings universal to motherhood."
Celeste Palermo, author
The Coffee Mom's Devotional and *From the Red Tees*

"Sarah Smiley's frank writing offers an atypical perspective of military life ... even those completely unfamiliar with life as a military spouse will relate and appreciate her witty accounts of being a wife and raising three children."
Bernie Grimm, Fox News legal analyst

I'm Just Saying...

For my guys
Dustin, Ford, Owen and Lindell
who provide the best writing material of all

I'm Just Saying...

TABLE OF CONTENTS

I'm Just Saying...

I'm Just Saying...

Foreword

I met Sarah Smiley two years ago when we were developing a TV pilot together based on her book *Going Overboard*. I had read Sarah's columns, and I was immediately smitten. The two of us couldn't have more different lives, and yet I was drawn to her stories about being a military wife and working mom.

Sarah has that unique ability as a writer to take the small moments of everyday life and see the universal in them. And that's why I feel she has struck such a chord with the public. Her columns are always clever, oh so witty and thought-provoking.

The best thing about Sarah is that she is someone who walks the talk. She is as hands-on as a mom can be to Ford, Owen and Lindell and a loving and affectionate wife to Dustin. All that, AND a career as a writer. I must also give major props to Dustin, as he would take the reins of the boys when Sarah and I needed to work with complete and unwavering confidence. (Not like so many dads I know, who after just two minutes with the kids come looking for their wife like a lost puppy dog!)

So I can guarantee the reader that they will love this book. It is a true talent to mine your own life and find gold. And with Sarah Smiley at the helm, the results are fourteen karat.

~ Carol Leifer

I'm Just Saying...

Foreword

As the editor of Military.com, I have the privilege of reading Sarah's column a couple of days before the rest of the world each week. And it feels like a privilege because her voice is distinct not just among military spouses who write for large audiences, but also among writers, period. In Sarah's writing you will find humor, wit, joy, frustration—the full range of elements associated with working "the toughest job in the military" (to paraphrase what used to be printed on commissary grocery bags). But, more importantly, you'll also find the truth. And that's a gift few who put pen to paper, regardless of genre, can offer.

Sarah is among those rare talents who defy labels. She's self-deprecating, but rightly proud. You could call her a humorist, but you'd miss her pointed criticism. You could call her a critic, but you'd miss how she loves her life. And I dare you to try and guess what she's going to write about next. (Go ahead; give it a try.)

Although military families will certainly warm to Sarah's observations here, a reader doesn't need military experience to relate to them. In Dustin lives every well-meaning-but-sometimes-bumbling husband, not just those who fly Navy helicopters for a living. Owen, Ford and Lindell are not just military dependents; they're typical kids. And Sarah's not just a Navy wife; she's the glue holding this 21st Century family—this beautiful mess that might live in Ocala, Fla., as readily as it lives aboard Naval Air Station Oceana—together.

So enjoy this collection of essays. In them you'll find the modern military, America and yourself.

~ Ward Carroll

I'm Just Saying...

Introduction

They told me that syndication is dead. "No one does that anymore," they said. "Not if your name isn't Dave Barry."

But I had nothing to lose. My name isn't Dave Barry. I was a young mother with a home-again/gone-again military-pilot husband, and well, if Uncle Sam had control over everything else in our lives—from my husband's haircut to our family's zip code—he sure as heck wasn't going to keep me from having a career. Writing is my first love, and as I saw it, my only shot at having something of my own (very important for military spouses). Plus, I was mad at my husband, Dustin, for reasons about which you will soon read, and I do all sorts of crazy things when I'm mad at Dustin.

I called *The Washington Post* the next day.

"Hi, my name is Sarah Smiley," I said. "I write a column for my local newspaper, and I was wondering if you might like to publish it, too."

There was a giggle on the other end. My heart pounded. I felt like a knobby-kneed kid standing at the end of the high-dive. Suddenly I had this fear, like in a bad dream, that I was on speakerphone. I pictured the newsroom stopping in the middle of their work, then slapping their knees and bending over with laughter when they realized that I wasn't kidding.

"That's really cute," the nice editor said. "But no, we're not interested. Best of luck to you."

I heard the usual noise of a newsroom in the background and felt relieved that at least my request and the editor's answer probably had not been broadcast throughout the *Post*.

I put aside my dream to have my column in more than just one newspaper.

I'm Just Saying...

Once, when I was about 11 years old, I came up with what I thought was an excellent idea for a new board game. I created a prototype, wrote up a proposal, and sent the package to Parker Brothers. The company sent back a very nice note telling me that they had all the new ideas they could handle for awhile. Judging by their fast reply, however, I can only assume that my proposal never got past the secretary. Maybe not even the postman. Back then, as with the *Post*, I had a sense that my board game, made entirely with poster board, magic markers and scotch tape, was left in the break room at Parker Brothers for everyone to laugh at.

But they *had* replied, hadn't they? And I didn't die from embarrassment.

I remembered this a few weeks after my chat with the *Post* editor. I decided to try again. Only this time, I would work myself up to the high-dive.

I called the *Times-Record* in Brunswick, Maine. They accepted my offer, and just like that, I was finally in more than one newspaper.

Over the next six months, I continued to acquire new positions at newspapers around the country, until eventually my column was reaching two million readers (surprisingly, most of them civilian) weekly.

The moral of this story: Great things come from being mad at Dustin.

~ Sarah Smiley

I'm Just Saying...

MARRIAGE

DUSTIN:

HE LEAVES HIS LUNCH ON
THE ROOF OF HIS CAR.

THE DOLL SAYS
THAT ROOM IS HERS

Some people are afraid of clowns. I get that. These people don't go to the circus, and they don't hire clowns for their child's birthday party. Other people are afraid of birds, thanks to the 1963 Alfred Hitchcock movie. They avoid aviaries and don't buy pets with feathers. My husband, Dustin, the highly educated military pilot trained for combat, is afraid of something else. Dustin is afraid of baby dolls.

"I don't like the way they stare at me," Dustin says, adding that he thinks dolls switch places and run around the place, possibly with knives, each time he leaves a room, only to get back into their original position when he returns.

Dustin is especially afraid of antique dolls, the kind that have blinking eyes and are losing some of their wiry hair. Unfortunately for him, my grandmother in Missouri has truckloads of these dolls. We stayed at Grandma's house last week while she was in the hospital recovering from a heart attack, which was not doll-related.

In the living room, Grandma has two new life-size dolls that are held up in a standing position with metal braces that my son Ford, 6, observed were "going up the doll's bottom." This is how Dustin was greeted upon entering the house. I saw him shudder. But we were with my dad, a retired admiral and once my husband's active-duty superior, so Dustin had to pretend that the dolls didn't bother him. He bravely walked past one that came up to his knees.

My mom, an antiques collector, also has an impressive (or, "gruesome" if you are like Dustin) array of old, plastic dolls scattered around her house in Virginia. Some of the doll's heads are loose and wobble on their necks. A few of the blinking eyes are stuck closed; the others just look cross-eyed. Most of my mom's collection is so old, the plastic is sticky and there are exposed "pores" on the scalp where clumps of hair have fallen out. There was at least one occasion when my mom traded dolls with another collector on eBay, and a set was shipped with the heads in one box and the headless bodies in another. Dustin looks like he will pass out every time my mom retells that story.

But for the most part, my mom is sensitive to Dustin's fear, and she hides the dolls whenever we are visiting. Then, Dustin opens the closet to put away his clothes and finds a pile of naked dolls with their heads twisted sideways, or worse, backwards, staring at him from the top shelf. He doesn't find this nearly as funny as my mom and I do. In any case, given the fact that most people shield Dustin from baby dolls, he was taken off guard by all the "staring dolls" in my grandmother's house.

"Your room will be the first one on the right," my mom said as Dustin came through the living room with another load of suitcases. Dustin turned to enter the room and said, "Oh, God!" There was a pile of baby dolls on the bed, each of them staring up at him even though their bodies were facing a different direction. Dustin resolved to be brave ... and perhaps employ things he'd learned at SERE (Survival, Evasion, Resistance, and Escape) school. He would not mention the pile to anyone else.

About an hour later, I went with my mom, dad and the kids to the grocery store. Dustin stayed behind to do work. As we were pulling out of the driveway, I had a vision of Dustin bound and gagged in my grandmother's basement. The dolls, of course, would be back in their original places.

When we got back from the store, Dustin was tired (presumably from fighting off dolls), so he headed off to bed. While he was brushing his teeth, my mom took pity on him and moved the dolls. Only she forgot one waist-high girl standing in the corner next to the bed.

Dustin finished in the bathroom, said goodnight to everyone, and went into the room Mom had said was "his." He closed the bedroom door. A few minutes later, Dustin ran back into the living room like a kid running away from an imaginary monster in the middle of the night. By this point he didn't care that my dad was there or that he himself is a grown man. He sat down on the couch, hugged his knees to his chest, and said, "The doll says that room is hers."

No, Not That Chick-Fil-A!

The biggest difference between little boys and little girls is birthday parties. Think pink princesses versus G.I. Joe.

And the difference between grown-up (I use the term loosely) boys and grown-up girls?

How they plan for children's birthday parties.

Ford and Owen, my two little angels—angels who like to throw sticks and eat dirt—recently celebrated their fifth and third birthdays. Because their birthdays are only 72 hours apart, and also because my husband, Dustin, is cheap and I'm lazy, we have one party for both boys. This makes things easy on everyone, especially me, but there still is that issue of agreeing on a party theme. This year, as always, my vote was for Sesame Street. Ford and Owen wanted to do Batman and Superman for the third year in a row. But I'm in the midst of a parental dilemma (caused mostly by the strange looks other mothers at preschool give me when Ford speaks of his "Bat-gadgets"), so I've put a temporary halt to the superhero paraphernalia. We agreed on a pirate theme, which besides the swords and references to swashbuckling, is a kinder, gentler birthday party, don't you think?

Oh, who am I kidding? The pirate thing is probably just as bad, if not worse, than Batman and his nunchucks. But, in any case, I told the boys that they could have a pirate birthday party so long as it was at Chick-fil-A. Why Chick-fil-A tempers the pirate theme, I'm not sure. Maybe it has something to do with the restaurant being closed on Sundays.

I booked the party for Saturday at the Chick-fil-A on Highway 90 (remember that because it's important ... which is the same thing

I told Dustin). A very pleasant employee, after telling me it was "her pleasure" to schedule the party, promptly asked, "Do you want the big cow to visit?"

I know what you're thinking. How could anyone pass up an offer like that? Well, apparently not me, because I booked the "big cow," not realizing he is an added expense (you'll see why later). But if my boys are going to swing swords at their friends, the least I can do is offer a Chick-fil-A cow.

The day of the party, I left the house early to pick up the birthday cake. Before leaving, I said over and over again to Dustin, "Make sure the boys are at the Chick-fil-A on Highway 90 at 11 o'clock. Do I need to write it down? You won't forget, will you? It's not the Chick-fil-A by Target; it's the one on Highway 90. And don't forget to bring the camera, too."

"How dumb do I look?" Dustin said.

I left only slightly reassured that my husband and children would arrive on time and at the right Chick-fil-A.

If you're a regular reader of this column, you know where this is headed.

Fifteen minutes into the party, with children (none of them the birthday boys) pawing at the cake and an employee insisting it would be her "pleasure to bring out the big cow any time," Dustin called from his cell phone and said, "The good news is that I remembered the camera. The bad news is that I'm at the wrong Chick-fil-A."

This was a moment Dustin will never forget.

For the rest of his life.

But time goes on, and there are "big cows" to see, so I put on my party-mom face and tried not to look like I wanted to bang my husband's head with Batman's nunchucks.

After the birthday boys arrived, chicken nuggets were consumed and lemonades slurped down, I told the employee, "bring on the cow." And lo and behold, five minutes later, I learned why the "big cow" is an added expense: no grown-up would put on that costume for free. There in the doorway of the kitchen and headed for our table was a seven-foot cloth cow with "Eat More Chicken" spray-painted on his belly. Children cried and ran for their mother's legs. I couldn't blame them. Batman and his gadgets probably would have been less disturbing. To the cow's credit, he did give the kids high-fives and passed out ice cream, but still, more than a few children couldn't get over the vision of a black-and-white beast walking upright on its hind legs.

Now, I'm not saying I'm against the big cow or that I wouldn't use him again. He is part of the Chick-fil-A experience, after all. My only regret is not making Dustin dress up in the cow costume instead. Why, it would have been my pleasure to pay even more money just for that.

Dustin Smiley Forgets To Shave His Legs

Did you know that as recently as the 1970s, it was believed that a service member's spouse's participation (read: "reputation") was a factor in considering military promotions?

Ah, but here's the real shocker: according to some people, this practice continues today, albeit in a more discreet, elusive sort of way. Don't believe it? Don't worry, I'm not sure I believe it either. I mean, Dustin's made it this far, hasn't he?

Even so, here's what a retired Navy reader recently sent me via email after one of my finger-pointing columns about military medicine:

A word to the wise: in my day not all the inputs considered by promotion boards were written down … you may want to wash soiled linen within the service in order to preclude a future whine about the promotion process.

I receive this type of sentiment a lot, actually. One of the most frequently asked questions about my column is "Your husband lets you write that?" Coincidentally, there is also a heated debate on Military.com's message board titled, "Reflection of our spouses?" where military spouses are arguing back and forth about whether or not our actions—our lives—can affect our spouse's image within the military.

To put an end to the bickering, I've decided to pose a little scientific study. Let's say I asked this question, "If I, Sarah Smiley, am merely a reflection on my spouse and not a separate human being, who by the way, happens to be a civilian … ," (remember this is very scientific) "then it is safe to assume the following:

Dustin Smiley forgets to shave his legs every other day.

Dustin Smiley dyed his hair blonde, but thought it looked fake, so he's gone back to brown.

Dustin Smiley wishes he could remember that it takes two-thirds cup of water to make microwave macaroni and cheese, but, alas, he has to read the small print on the back of the box every single time.

Dustin Smiley gets a giant blister on his right toe when he wears his favorite red high heels.

Dustin Smiley always gets the loud shopping cart with the lopsided wheels.

Dustin Smiley still hasn't figured out how to do the "self check-out" at Wal-Mart.

Dustin Smiley is trying to lose weight, but a love for chocolate frosting is proving that to be difficult.

Dustin Smiley rarely showers before he takes the kids to school in the morning.

Dustin Smiley is afraid of mice.

Dustin Smiley nearly threw out his shoulder trying on one of those fancy girdles with the nice new name, "Spanx."

Dustin Smiley's greatest fear is being trapped in a public bathroom stall, because he'd rather sit there and starve than crawl on the floor underneath to get out.

Dustin Smiley's favorite spectator sport is bull riding, although this has less to do with the "sport," and more to do with the riders.

Dustin Smiley is trying to cut back to only two Diet Dr. Peppers a day, which is only causing him to eat more chocolate frosting.

When Dustin Smiley is nervous, he grinds his teeth so hard that his nose gets numb.

Dustin Smiley feels cranky in the morning if his pants are too tight, his underwear too large, or if his hair looks like someone hit him over the head with a frying pan.

Dustin Smiley mistakenly believes he has a good voice when he sings "Gilligan's Island" in the shower.

Nothing says home to Dustin Smiley like a nice pair of leopard print slippers and flannel pajamas.

Dustin Smiley once tried to count to a million and threw up.

And last, Dustin Smiley married a fantastic spouse!

So judging by our little experiment, I think it's safe to say just one thing: Dustin Smiley's wife has issues.

As for all this reflecting-on-our-spouses stuff? Well, I just hope the reverse isn't true (that our husbands reflect upon us), because that would mean that I'm terrible with directions and that I have a five o'clock shadow by noon.

Dustin And The Chinese Finger Lock

Last week, my husband's squadron had a Hail and Farewell party. A Hail and Farewell is the Navy's two-birds-with-one-stone answer to our transient lifestyle. At one party, we hail (welcome) and farewell (say goodbye to) all the families who are coming and going.

Isn't it just like the military to be so efficient?

Unlike other traditions in the military, however, there is no standard for Hail and Farewells. Venues and formalities run the gamut. Sometimes the event is held at a bar on a Saturday night. Sometimes it is held at a park, and families come with children in tow. Sometimes it is combined with another squadron function (a holiday party, for example) to maximize efficiency.

Last week's party was held at a restaurant inside a local bowling alley. The children were invited.

There was a time before I was pregnant, when an evening spent at a Hail and Farewell party meant this for me: I would spend hours gabbing with my spouse-club friends, drink too much wine, and come home with a smile on my face. But the bowling alley, coupled with my pregnancy and the children clinging to my leg, gave last week's party an entirely different feel. Instead of coming home with the musty smell of a night-out on my clothes and in my hair, I left the festivities early to bowl with my children. Shortly after the commanding officer had given his customary speeches, I exchanged my strappy red heels for purple bowling shoes and a pair of my six-year-old son's sweaty socks. Then, with pregnant belly and all, I proceeded to hurl an 11-pound bowling ball down the lane, while my husband watched and laughed.

I am so glad that no one had a camera.

Bowling didn't last long.

Next we went to the adjacent arcade, where I found my true passion and the only sport at which I excel: Skee Ball. I am so good at this game, I've been known to leap over small children at Chuck E. Cheese's when a lane at the Skee Ball machine becomes available. I'm also my family's designated skee-baller. When the boys want an expensive prize they'll never gain enough tickets for on their own, they call me for help. This night was no different. Over and over again, I rolled the skee ball up the ramp as the tickets came out of the machine like a tongue, folding onto themselves on the floor.

Dustin asked, "Are you close to winning the boys the life-size Batman?"

But you need around 3,000 tickets for the most coveted prizes—prizes that would only cost $2.00 at Wal-Mart—so I was no where near winning the life-size Batman.

After an unsuccessful night of Skee Ball (I blame the pregnancy), I only had enough tickets to win my boys a couple of plastic skeletons and one of those Chinese finger traps (you put a finger into the ends of the wicker tube and pull, and then—what fun!—your fingers are stuck).

On our way out to the parking lot, Dustin was noticeably agitated beside me. Out of the corner of my eye, I saw him struggling with something, but I was too busy making sure our boys didn't get run over by passing vehicles to pay attention.

Then, Dustin said in a panic, "Are you going to help get my fingers out of this thing, or do I have to live like this forever?"

He was stuck in the finger trap.

The boys started to cry, "Mommy, can you save him? Hurry, Mommy!"

I released Dustin's cinched fingers from the toy. His face was flushed. He looked scared.

"I would have had to wear this same shirt for the rest of my life if you hadn't set me free," he said. "I really didn't think I'd get my fingers out of there."

Then (are you ready for this?) like the true caveman that he is, Dustin put his fingers back into the trap to demonstrate for us how stuck he was.

I'm Just Saying...

Right then, I thought back on my night—how Dustin had sipped beer and laughed at me bowling pregnant—and there was a moment, however brief, that I considered leaving my husband with his fingers stuck in the Chinese finger trap.

One Gift, Two Holidays

Several years ago, Dustin gave me a Home Depot gift card for Christmas. Needless to say, a gift card from Home Depot was not exactly at the top of my wish list.

I had done everything except hire a skywriter to make Dustin aware of the gift I really wanted: a pearl pendant necklace. I circled the necklace in catalogs. I taped notes to the bathroom mirror. I wrote down the SKU number, item number, price and location on an index card and put it next to the telephone. Oh, how I had hoped for that necklace!

So you can imagine my excitement on Christmas morning when Dustin came to me with a small square box wrapped in red shiny paper. I tore off the ribbon, threw back the top, and there nestled in a rumpled bed of tissue paper was a gift card from Home Depot.

"Is this a joke?" I asked Dustin.

It wasn't a joke.

Dustin's face was pure innocence. "I thought you could use the gift card to buy floor tiles, and then I can remodel the porch," he said.

Oh yes, the porch floor, the one I had been asking him to fix. Now it all made sense! After months of asking him again and again about the floor, he finally decided to wrap it up for me, in the form of a Home Depot gift card.

Suddenly I recalled Christmases past, such as the year Dustin gave me a "Saturday Night Live" DVD that he wanted to watch. Or the year he gave me a jewelry box he had bought at a garage sale; when the bottom drawer of the jewelry box was opened, it played the theme song from "The Godfather," which at that time Dustin was watching from start to finish in marathon sessions.

Later, once our company was gone and the children were asleep, I asked Dustin, "Did you really think I'd want a Home Depot gift card?"

He really did.

"Had you totally overlooked the clues I dropped about the necklace?"

He hadn't. In fact, Dustin knew very well that I wanted the necklace. When pressed for a reason why he chose the gift card over the necklace, this was Dustin's exact quote: "The necklace just seemed so girly."

Just in case you are confused, yes, I am a girl.

Somewhere between that unforgettable answer and going to sleep very angry, I realized that our digital camera was not in its usual spot. It turned out that Dustin had left the camera outside…on top of the car…in the rain.

For New Year's a few days later, Dustin gave me a new digital camera.

This holiday, Dustin and I have agreed not to give each other gifts, which is always a tricky situation that feels a bit like a duel. I mean, what if I buy nothing for Dustin and then he gives me a bracelet? What if I live up to my end of the deal, but he gives me a new computer? What if he is only bluffing?

Except this is Dustin, my military-pilot-husband trained for war, not for shopping. Dustin might never live down the gift card/digital camera debacle, but that doesn't mean he hasn't tried (bless his heart). Last Christmas, in spite of my femininity, Dustin ditched the home-improvement stores and decided to give me something a little more, well, girly. He surprised me with a diamond anniversary band, and it was more beautiful than all the shiny bolts, levelers and hammers at Home Depot and Lowe's combined. Unfortunately, the ring was also too big. It had to be sent away and resized.

I waited more than a month for my ring to return, and on February 14 (Valentine's Day, imagine that!) there was a knock on the door. The UPS man handed me a small brown box with the jeweler's return address marked on it. I called Dustin at work to tell him the happy news.

"My ring came back today, and it is perfect," I said.

"Sweet," he said. "It came today? So, uh, Happy Valentine's Day then, too."

Five months later, on our anniversary, instead of exchanging gifts, Dustin asked me to look at my beautiful ring again and to recall all the happy surprises it had brought, not once, but twice—on Christmas and then again on Valentine's Day.

Hey, if a bad memory, such as the Home Depot gift card, can last for years and years and years, why not a happy memory, too? At least that's what Dustin said.

List For Getting Along
Causes Major Argument

Soon after Dustin and I married, we ran into a little snafu. First, I erupted in tears whenever Dustin failed to notice my house decorating skills or how clean I kept the bath towels. Dustin was angry that I didn't appreciate our tidy finances or the fact that he was working so hard in flight school. Apparently we were sensitive about the other not recognizing—or, worse, criticizing—what we considered to be our finer traits and talents. I called Dustin "cheap." He thought I was neurotic. Something had to be done.

So I decided that each of us should make a list of things that are critical to our self-worth, areas of talents or personality where one should tread lightly if they intend to criticize. It would be the official rules for "fighting fair." For instance, I take no pride in my cooking. It is fair game for Dustin's unrestrained criticism. But when it comes to my writing, my parenting skills, and my housekeeping, Dustin should choose his words carefully and dote when possible.

I knew Dustin's repertoire of jokes and his do-it-yourself home repairs would be on his list of perceived talents. But perhaps I hadn't made myself abundantly clear. You see, the spirit of this exercise was for us to choose only a handful of things. On the night we revealed our lists, I handed Dustin a short piece of paper with mine. What Dustin whipped out of his pocket looked like one of those accordion-style plastic wallets that hold a hundred pictures. I scanned his list. "You think you're a good singer?" I asked. "You can't be serious! And I can't make fun of the way you talk? This just won't do! You need to shorten your list."

One by one, I crossed items off Dustin's list. "You've left nothing for me to be mad at," I said. And then I blamed his mother for letting him believe he is the best at everything.

The activity ended in a fight, though we eventually got Dustin's list down to a manageable size. One of the items that remained was "do-it-yourself home repairs."

Fast forward to last month. Dustin was working on a stone pathway in our backyard. He spent three consecutive weekends on the project. Yet when I finally did a test-walk while he was at work, it was like teetering on the rocky shores of the Pacific. I had to put out both arms for balance. Even our son said, "Someone's going to break a leg on this."

But how could I tell Dustin? He had worked so hard. And he was so proud! Plus, "home repairs" was on his list. For several days I considered ways to give him a hint. I faked a fall on the path while he was watching. He just called out, "you OK?" I tried saying, "It looks kind of, um, rocky, doesn't it? Rocky is beautiful, but ... "

The message wasn't getting through. I resigned myself to accepting the treacherous path and walking on the grass if I was wearing anything else except hiking boots.

Then one night I asked Dustin to read my column for the next week. I was in our bedroom with the laptop and he was in our office with the desktop. I sent him an Instant Message (how high-tech couples communicate under the same roof these days) that read, "I'm forwarding my column to you. Tell me your thoughts."

A few minutes later Dustin replied: "The column is really bad. I don't like it at all. You should use something else."

Here I had been protecting his feelings—his manhood—for several weeks while twisting my ankle this way and that walking on the stone path, and he just threw a dagger at my heart like that.

I sent him another message. "Yeah, well, the path you made looks like (words my editors won't let me use)!"

The next weekend, Dustin relayed this story to a friend, only he described my "vicious" attack over Instant Message as "out of the blue" and "without provocation."

What can I say? My husband isn't the most observant or insightful person around. Although, come to think of it, I think those are on his list.

Giving Thanks For Dustin.
No, Really.

Dustin has often said that if I write too many positive stories about him, people will quit reading this column.

In the spirit of giving thanks this Thanksgiving week, however, I'm willing to take a chance so that I can tell you about just one of the ways Dustin takes care of yours truly.

Dustin is a military pilot trained for war, not sensitivity and domesticity. Readers might remember the time Dustin gave me a Home Depot gift card for Christmas, or the time he took the kids to the wrong restaurant for their birthday party. I've enjoyed picking on him for all the times he has left lunches, backpacks and groceries on top of the car. But Dustin may be at his best when I am making my own mistakes. Dustin teases that I am like a tornado, and he is the man with a broom cleaning up the mess. Often his teasing is figurative, but sometimes it seems literal, or, to be more accurate, financial. Two weeks ago, Dustin cleaned up all three.

The five of us—Dustin, our three boys and I—were staying in a hotel 45 miles away from home because I was speaking at a conference that began early in the morning. While I showered and reviewed my notes, Dustin took the boys to Waffle House. I was having a leisurely time, enjoying the quiet of the hotel room, when coming out of the shower and putting on my lotion, I realized that my face was red and irritated.

I'll have to spend a lot of time on my makeup this morning, I thought. That's when my gut sank to my knees and my eyes flew open. That's when I realized that I had forgotten every bit of my makeup at home.

When Dustin and the boys returned from breakfast, I was panicked. "You look fine without makeup," Dustin said, earning himself the first bonus point.

However, in about an hour, I'd be on stage talking to a crowd of 400 people. Going without makeup was possible, but not ideal. Dustin saw the fear on my blotchy face, and without further hesitation, loaded all of us in the car, drove me to the nearest mall, and waited outside with the kids while I bought all new makeup. It was a very expensive mistake.

Dustin never made me feel guilty. He circled the parking lot of the auditorium while I put on my new face. Then he kissed me goodbye and took the boys to ride go-karts while I went inside for my speaking engagement.

On the way home from the conference, I promised Dustin that I would make an effort to be more organized in the future. But I couldn't have known then that just three days later, my brother would visit and bring me an acoustic guitar, an item that would consume all my attention for the next several weeks. While I sat in the living room trying to apply my knowledge of the piano to the strings of the guitar, I let the family's clean laundry pile up on the bedroom floor until it was a mountain almost two feet tall. I'm not kidding.

One night, Ford was on his way to Cub Scouts and couldn't find the socks to his uniform. Looking back, I guess it might have seemed lazy or not helpful that I sat on the couch and played the guitar while Dustin looked under beds and seat cushions in search of the socks. Honestly, I sat there out of resignation. The pile of laundry seemed insurmountable; the socks a lost cause.

Suddenly, I heard Dustin yelling in a strained voice from the bedroom: "Wait a minute … I think I've … hold on … I've got something … " He was overly dramatic, of course, trying to make a point about the laundry. But then he appeared in the doorway, and I couldn't help but laugh. He had piled layers of socks, undershirts, underwear and gym shorts on his shoulders and head. He looked as if he had barely escaped the laundry alive. Then he held up Ford's socks and said, "It was a close call, but finally I got them."

I'm Just Saying...

Our house and our clothes might not be clean at all times. We might be forgetful when it comes to packing. And sometimes we leave things on top of the car and drive away. But this week, I am thankful that Dustin and I can clean up each other's messes and still maintain enough energy—and love—to laugh about it later.

Palma, Spain, Makes Dustin Smile

Mention Palma, Spain, and my husband's eyes light up. He himself cannot say the words without the corners of his mouth literally curling into a smile. He tries to hide it, like someone swallowing back a yawn, but it is obvious. Dustin remembers the island in Spain with as much passion as someone remembering their first kiss.

Palma, Spain, was my husband's first port-call on his first six-month deployment. Perhaps sailors always remember their first port-call with fondness, but Dustin's joy is excessive and sorely misplaced. You see, Dustin made one horrible mistake in Palma: He called me— drunk. He had not yet learned the art of calling your wife as soon as you get on dry land but before you've had a good time.

There I was in my bed when the phone rang and I heard my husband's voice for the first time in weeks. Behind him, I also heard the steady beat of music and the hoots and hollers of people having a good time. I had been waiting for his call for so long. I had been dreaming of what we'd say to one another. I had a whole list of questions and things I wanted to tell him. But as soon as Dustin called me "Babe," I knew he was drunk. Our conversation was headed no where good. I regret to admit that I hung up on my husband that night.

However, despite all of this, six years later, the word Palma still brings a smile to Dustin's face, which elicits an immediate jab in the side from me.

I recounted this episode in my memoir, *Going Overboard: The Misadventures of a Military Wife* (Penguin/NAL 2005), and the passage has evoked a lot of responses from readers. Apparently there are three types of military wives: those who revel in their spouse's port-call enjoyment ("He deserves all the fun and relaxation," they say); those who dread port-calls ("He's visiting all these fun places while I'm stuck at home with the kids? No fair!"); and finally, those who are glad for their husbands, but don't want to hear about it ("Have fun, don't call me drunk, and bring home some pearls, would ya?").

There is this same polarization at Spouse Club meetings when the ship is about to pull into port. Half the spouses dread the obvious comparison between their husband's foreign travels and their own homebound life. The other half scolds the first half for not having compassion for their spouse's hard work and much-earned liberty. In my time as a military wife, I've felt both of these emotions equally, and often at the same time.

Yes, our spouses are working hard, defending our freedom and earning a living, but that doesn't make staying home any easier. Despite the pride we have in our spouses, it's difficult knowing that he's eating exotic cuisine and drinking fine wine when you're hauling the kids to tee-ball practice and unsuccessfully potty training a three year old. Our rational brains tell us on thing, our emotional brains another. That's OK. It's perfectly human to feel like you will spit nails when your husband tells you all the Spanish women are beautiful, as my husband did that night. This doesn't make you a bad wife or unfit to be a military spouse. (For the record, however, Dustin's behavior on the phone was decidedly not "perfectly human," but rather a little piggish.)

Some readers were upset—or, "appalled," rather—that I hung up on Dustin. Fear not, he had already had too many drinks for my boldness to have the impact I desired. (Later Dustin admitted that he would have hung up on him, too.)

After all this, you may be wondering why Dustin still smiles when he thinks of Palma. For the answer, please revisit the above pig comment. Then remember that the first port-call is a rite of passage for sailors, something that an angry wife can't take away.

But I'm not that bitter anymore. Really, I'm not. After all, Dustin brought home some nice Majorca pearl earrings for me. And yes, he smiles every time I wear them ... because they make him think of Spain.

Melted Pacifiers
Make Dustin A Hero

I spend a lot of time making fun of my husband, Dustin, the highly trained Navy pilot who continually drives off with things—coffee cups, lunch bags, grocery sacks—on the roof of his car. Today, I'm taking it all back.

Last week Dustin was cooking a hotdog on the stove, and I was cooking pacifiers right next to him. No, wait; let me rephrase that. I was supposed to be boiling pacifiers, because that's what you do to clean them. We'll get back to the "cooking" part in a minute.

Why was I boiling pacifiers for my third child? Shouldn't I just lick them and pop them back into his mouth? On a good day, yes. But on this day, my older boys, Ford, 6, and Owen, 4, had actually stepped on one of Lindell's pacifiers and accidentally dragged it across the ground pressed between the garage floor and the soles of their shoes. After three kids, I can deal with many things, but not a baby's pacifier sandwiched between the floor and a dirty sneaker.

So I was cooking—no, boiling—the pacifiers in a pan, while Dustin cooked a hotdog in a skillet. Dustin sat down for lunch, and I joined him at the table. We talked about our day while I continued to cook—no, boil!—the pacifiers. When Dustin was finished, he left to mow the lawn, and I got busy cleaning dishes. When I passed by the stove, I noticed a hot, electric smell and found the hotdog skillet sizzling with nothing but grease inside. The bottom was completely scorched, with two long black lines where the hotdogs had been.

I turned off the stove and marched outside. I wanted to give Dustin "the look"—and by "look," of course, I mean the you-who-always-messes-up-everything look. Dustin released the blade control on the mower, looked at my scowl and said, "What?" with all the innocence of a child.

"You never turned off the stove, that's what. And now you've scorched the bottom of the skillet."

Dustin looked surprised. "Oh, I must have turned off the water for the pacifiers instead."

I marched back inside.

"Sorry," Dustin called out behind me.

I turned on the stove for the pacifiers and began cooking—yes, cooking—them again. Only I didn't know I was cooking them at the time, so I went to take a shower. Then I put on makeup, dried my hair, got dressed, and because nobody was yelling "Mom, can you come put Batman's cape back on for us" yet, and Dustin was still outside mowing the lawn, I did really important things like pluck my eyebrows, clip cuticles off my nails, and suck in my cheeks like a fish to see what I'd look like with liposuction.

All of the sudden, I heard a clattering sound in the kitchen. Dustin ran through the house screaming, "Sarah! Sarah!"

I came out of the bedroom. Black smoke billowed down the hallway and licked at the ceiling. Dustin ran past me with a smoking saucepan. He set it on the front porch, and then he started yelling for everyone to get out of the house. I sat with the boys outside while Dustin went around opening windows and doors. When I peered into the saucepan, there was a thick layer of liquid latex bubbling in the bottom.

I had cooked the pacifiers.

The inside of our house smelled like a burning tire factory for several hours, and I had to go to the store to get Lindell new pacifiers. Dustin never said a word. How easily he could have said, "Little miss come-out-and-yell-at-me-for-the-scorched-skillet!" How justified he would have been to lay into me for being so careless. Instead, he just took care of it: running fans, spraying deodorizer and vacuuming the carpets.

"Thank you for being so nice to me about this," I said later that night.

And Dustin said, "Well, I would have wanted someone to be nice to me."

We agreed that when we are both old and senile, we will need a really good fire extinguisher in the kitchen.

The next morning, as I was throwing away the ruined saucepan, I thought to myself, maybe I should stop teasing Dustin so much and start being thankful that he's mine.

Men:

THEY ARE LIKE WOMEN. ONLY DIFFERENT.

Always Keep Your Fat Clothes

There's only one thing worse than the thought of trying on old clothes that you wore 10 years and 20 pounds ago. That being, of course, actually trying on old clothes that you wore 10 years and 20 pounds ago. My closet is filled with every size from 2 to 14, thanks to my previous stages of pregnancy, postpartum, youth and motherhood (although not necessarily in that order).

I'm not dumb; I know I will never fit into a size 2 again. Yet I hang on to a dozen dresses that look like they could fit a large cat, because it gives me a sick feeling of happiness to see them and realize that I once wore those tiny dresses, some of them even while I was six-months pregnant with my first child.

I hang on to the larger dresses for the same reason: I'm not dumb. I know I will likely wear them again. But I never try on any dress from either end of the spectrum. The pharmaceutical companies haven't produce enough Xanax to get me into the dress I wore on the first date with my husband. It is emotionally damaging enough just to see the dress, with its telling layer of dust on the shoulders. I can hold the dress up by its hanger and actually feel the way the darts on the bust would reduce my chest to one big uni-boob, and the A-line skirt would look more like an "A" with an apple stuck inside of it.

No, I don't want to try these dresses on. I just want to know they are there.

Last week, Dustin and I were cleaning out our closet, and we came across a rack full of Dustin's old military uniforms. Some of them were from his days at the Naval Academy eleven years ago.

"You're not keeping those, are you?" I said.

"You don't think they'll fit me?" he asked.

It's true that Dustin's body has changed significantly less than mine in the ten years that we've been married. He has not, after all, had an 8-pound human being inside him. Nonetheless, I knew that his old white uniform pants wouldn't fit him anymore than my wedding dress would still fit me.

"No, I don't think they will fit you," I said. "Put them in the give-away pile."

"Give-away? These aren't give-aways," he said. "I always need uniform pants."

"You need uniform pants that fit."

"I think these will fit just fine," Dustin said, and he started to unbuckle his pants.

I realized then that males apparently are not equipped with the same sense that women have for judging how many seams they will bust when they attempt to put on old clothes. Dustin, God love him, really thought he could fit into those pants. Once he squeezed himself into them, however, the fabric was so taught, the hems drew up five inches above his ankles. His rear end was flattened like a pancake, and his stomach was pushed out of the waistband, like toothpaste coming out of a tube.

He looked like fat Elvis.

"See, they fit great," Dustin said.

Oh, but it gets worse. He continued to try on old uniform pants, including ones that were the same size as the first unsuccessful pair. Each time, he thought he looked great.

Then we found an old photo album from when were dating. We were shocked at how young we looked. The kids heard us laughing and came to see. "Look at Dad," they howled, pointing at the pictures. "He was so skinny! And look at all the hair he had!"

I reached over and squeezed Dustin's shoulder. "We've definitely changed," I said. "But I think I like us better now."

He agreed.

The next day, Dustin put all of his old uniform pants in a bag and took them to work to give away. He was braver than I am to try on his old clothes, even braver still to take them to his peers and admit they don't fit.

Although, for all his gumption, he did make one big mistake. He gave away all of his old clothes. He didn't even save one pair to hang in the back of the closet. You know what that means. Now his medium pants will become the smallest items in his closet, and because those fit even just a little, he'll always think he can have another slice of pie and a second helping of spaghetti. And then someday, those pants won't fit either.

Just as you might leave one dead ant on the floor as a warning for all of his ant friends, you should always leave at least one piece of thin clothes in your closet.

But you never—not ever—try it on.

Home Depot Reduces Men To Neanderthals

We just moved into a new house, which, oddly enough, means that I spend an inordinate amount of time at Home Depot, the home improvement store.

One would think that a new house doesn't need "improvements," yet I can't function in my normal life these days because I'm obsessed with improving our home, which was just built.

Admittedly, most of my need to quickly (as in RIGHT NOW!) set up house is rooted in my military upbringing. With only two to three years to live in a home, I feel pressured to get settled fast so we can maximize our enjoyment before the next move. And for reasons unknown to me, getting settled—into a newly constructed house, remember—requires daily trips to Home Depot, the home improvement store.

But I can't pretend I don't like my trips to Home Depot, because they've afforded me many lessons in the differences between men and women, which, since you asked, I will dispense now.

First, men walk into Home Depot with a purpose. They have serious, thoughtful looks on their faces as they wander aimlessly down aisles pretending to know where they are going or what they're looking for. Sometimes men shopping at Home Depot even frown, but I think this is just to make us women believe that shopping for tools is hard on a guy and that they don't get any enjoyment out of it at all.

I, on the other hand, walk into Home Depot as I do every other store—with a bewildered look on my face and a well-intended shopping list crumpled in my left hand. It doesn't matter if I'm shopping for earrings at Target or for a caulk gun at Home Depot, when I hear the clickety-clack of shopping cart wheels, my heart races and I am momentarily unaware of other things ... such as my bank account balance. This trance-like shopping state allows me to actually speak to and smile at other shoppers, which, if you'll notice, men at Home Depot never do. My friend Sonja and I met in one aisle and had a wonderful conversation about the difference between semi-gloss and satin paint finishes, while the men standing near us frowned at shiny green lawn mowers and tried to look really "busy."

Another difference between men and women at Home Depot is that men, for all the pained, serious looks on their faces, will always make shopping for hardware more difficult than it needs to be. While searching for a 5/16-inch cross dowel nut (whatever that is), Dustin would have rather let our dog chew a hole through the deck than ask an employee in an orange apron for help.

"It doesn't have to be this difficult," I said to Dustin. "Just ask someone for help."

But no, that would take the fun out of it.

Meanwhile, a man and his wife standing next to us were having nearly the same conversation. They were shopping for a tool bench and although the man was confused about which features came with which benches, he wouldn't take his wife's advice to ask for help. He was getting a lot more accomplished frowning at the display and rubbing his chin.

The man's wife looked on as he rapped the top of a wooden bench with his knuckles, because obviously at some point in his life he had learned that testing the sturdiness of a piece of wood involves only knocking on it like a front door. I also watched with curiosity because I have never in my experience known a 4-inch piece of solid wood to crumble beneath anyone's knuckles, and I seriously doubted that it was an effective way to evaluate a work bench.

After a while of this, and without Dustin noticing (which wasn't hard), I slipped away from aisle number 10 to find help. When I returned with a man in an orange apron, Dustin's face looked panicked. Now he'd actually have to talk to a human being in Home Depot!

So I was the one who asked the employee about cross dowel nuts, and when he said, "We don't have one that big because we're not a real hardware store, just a home improvement store," I thought Dustin's little heart would break.

But really, it makes sense, you know? I mean, why would a city filled with new homes need anything more than a store for home improvements?

Don't Ask, Don't Tell

Recently my husband and I had a dangerous conversation. It began with a question that can be described as nothing less than morbid curiosity: "Dustin, which of my friends are you most attracted to?"

Why do women ask these things? We want to know the answer about as badly as we want to hear about our neighbor's toe surgery. It's like watching a Cesarean section on TLC's "Baby Story" with one eye closed and one hand on the clicker, ready to flip the channel as soon as blood appears.

Military wives are the same way when asking questions about deployments.

"Do the women in Spain really go topless at the beach?"

"Are French women as beautiful as everyone says?"

"Do you have fun on deployment?"

Once, when Dustin called from overseas, I asked him, "Are you having a good time?" A reasonable outsider might think this was a genuine question and that I truly wanted to know the answer. So why did I start crying when he said, "I'm having the time of my life"?

Women ask these questions because secretly we want a certain response. Any man who's ever fallen prey to such inquiries as "Does this dress make me look fat?" or "Do you like my new haircut?" knows what I mean. It's a trap. What seems like a question is really a giant piece of cheese on the mousetrap that is female emotions. Go for the cheese and you spend the next few hours dying a miserable death. Avoid the cheese and the trap follows you around the house nagging, "Why won't you answer me? You think I look fat, don't you? Is this about your mother?" Before you know it, you're fighting about the insensitive card you gave her for her birthday last year, and you're not even sure why.

The absolute worst trap to fall for, however, is, "What are you thinking about?"

Never ever answer this question! Unless—and this is a very important caveat—your response is, "I'm thinking about how smart and beautiful you are."

One time, after a brief time apart, I met my returning husband at the door and asked, "What did you think about while you were away?"

And he said (I'm not kidding), "Actually, I was thinking about how big your head is."

I assumed he meant this figuratively and that he was alluding to arrogance and ego. I began to pout, and Dustin started back-peddling.

"No, wait! I don't mean it that way," he said. "I mean, I was really thinking about the physical size of your head. It's huge! Do you realize how big it is compared to your body?"

SNAP went the trap.

I stared at Dustin in disbelief, then I ran to the nearest bathroom to check the size of my head. As I cried in front of the mirror, Dustin begged for mercy. "But you asked what I was thinking about!"

You'd think I'd learn, but I continue to ask my husband agonizing questions and subsequently cry over my self-inflicted pain. I might never recover from the time I was pregnant with our first son and asked, "How have I changed the most?" Dustin had so many safe options—"Your hair is shinier," or "You're glowing"—but no, he said, "I think your butt has gotten bigger."

SNAP!

So which friend is my husband most attracted to? His answer shocked me. It was a girl I knew briefly during our first year of marriage and haven't seen since. The sting of his revelation was consoled only by this: Dustin admitted believing that my friend had a crush on him as well! A good jolly laugh at that and I was back to worrying about more important things. Like the size of my head.

Simple Tasks Are Hard For "Smart" Men

My interest in Dustin's brain piqued this past week when my son's backpack turned up at the local sheriff's department. As I signed away what I'm sure was my right arm to release the Thomas the Tank bag from police custody, I recounted the previous day's events and tried to remind myself that Dustin is a smart man.

We had just gotten home from church Wednesday night when I realized that we were missing Ford's backpack, a bag filled with diapers and matchbox cars, and everything else a mother needs to make the next morning run smoothly.

"Uh, technically we didn't leave the backpack at the church," said Dustin, who was looking rather nervous. "I think I left it on top of the car, so, uh, it's probably lying on the road somewhere."

I envisioned tire marks across poor Thomas's cheeky face. Then I made a mental note to call Michele, the church secretary, the next day to see if anyone turned in the bag.

This wasn't the first time Dustin had left something on the roof of our car. It also wasn't the first demonstration of his incredible memory ... er, lack of it. Dustin once called from work because he forgot his shoes and needed me to bring them. How does someone forget their shoes? Another time he took out a chunk of plaster from our garage wall with the side mirror of his truck because he forgot about the bike on the other side. But my favorite (I use the term loosely) was the time he unloaded the dishwasher and put all the plates and cups back in the cabinet—and the plates and cups were still dirty.

I'm Just Saying...

Did I mention that my husband is a highly trained Navy pilot? Yes, that's right. He can land a helicopter on the deck of a ship, but he can't remember to take restaurant leftovers off the top of the car.

My dad, another highly trained Navy pilot, is the same way. One time Dad pulled his car to the side of the road and got underneath to investigate a "suspicious noise." Dad, who has built car engines himself, was confused when the curious sound wouldn't stop. I don't even know how to check my own car's oil, but it didn't take me long to realize that the noise was Dad's cell phone ringing in the glove compartment. Dad can probably explain the entire concept of cellular communication, but I doubt he knows how to program phone numbers into a cell phone.

Which brings us back to Dustin leaving things on top of our car, a car whose engine he might be able to draw a diagram of.

Early Thursday morning, someone reported a child's backpack abandoned in the middle of the road. The sheriff's department came to investigate and took the item into custody. Twenty-four hours later I was driving to the city jail to release poor Thomas the Tank. After assuring a deputy that the backpack was in fact ours—a process that involved proving everything from my son's diaper size to the number of toy cars in his possession—they turned over the bag. It was sealed inside a large brown sack marked "EVIDENCE."

I've saved the evidence bag and placed it not so inconspicuously on a shelf in our garage. I hope it will serve as a reminder to my husband that (1) it was all his fault, and (2) despite being a very smart man, sometimes he still needs a lot of help.

Glasses Are ... Sexy?

Cancel the LASIK eye surgery, ladies. Glasses are sexy. This information comes from our local morning radio show. I was driving the other day when I heard the crew—one of those too-perky-for-seven-in-the-morning-ensembles consisting of two men and one woman—counting down the 10 sexiest ways women change their appearance. I turned up the volume and hushed the children because not only am I a married mother (read: I'm getting old), I also vowed my life to a man who would choose a good San Diego Padres game over most any other activity, if you know what I mean.

I could not let this information pass me by.

The first items on the list weren't surprising. The two men said that things like "no makeup," "messy" hair, and uncoordinated outfits are major turn-ons. Of course, by "no makeup," "messy" hair, and I-just-threw-this-together style, what these poor, unsuspecting men really mean, without realizing it, is that they like it when women wear really expensive makeup in just the right amount so that it looks like they are wearing nothing. They also like it when a woman spends time she could have used watching "The Today Show" teasing her hair, putting expensive goop in it, and making it look like she "just rolled out of bed." And they like it when we search high and low for the perfect pair of red heels to go with our green outfit because that would make it look oh-so "uncoordinated."

Men are so simple. Why isn't it this easy to trick my husband into believing that I didn't just spend $100 at Target today?

The items on the list closer to number one, however, were a little more surprising. The men said that a woman wearing dog tags, camouflage pants and her husband's button-down shirt (not necessarily all at the same time) is incredibly sexy. Yes, that's right, they want us to look like men. They also like tan lines, tattoos and big muscles. Whatever.

Just as I was beginning to count my blessings that I'm no longer in the dating world—because when I do the no-makeup, messy-hair, clothes-don't-match routine, it usually isn't on purpose—the morning team announced the number one sexiest thing women do to change their appearance.

Are you ready for this?

They wear glasses.

I could hardly believe my luck. I was just prescribed my first set of glasses last month (I went in for a "floater" and came out with glasses; at the time I thought this was bad news). I might truly sport no makeup, messy hair, baggy post-partum pants and 40 extra pounds, but by golly, I'm farsighted.

Somehow I don't think this—a disheveled mother of three schlepping around in her reading glasses—is what the men had in mind.

Still, I couldn't wait to tell Dustin the great news. When I bought my designer (read: much too expensive) glasses, Dustin grilled me for not choosing cheap military ones instead. Have you ever seen military-issued prescription glasses, otherwise known as "birth control"? They are horrible, boxy things that bring to mind my elementary-school gym teacher in polyester shorts. I don't know why. But I can assure you they wouldn't lure Dustin away from a good baseball game. I'm just saying.

"But they're cheap," Dustin said.

Coincidentally, just after receiving my glasses, I had an appointment with the gynecologist to discuss birth control options (because after you've had a baby, the first thing doctors want to know is how you will stop procreating in the future). I was tempted to say, "I'm just going to wear military-issued glasses," but I already had my super-cute designer pair (which I now know qualify as "sexy"—yay for me!), so the joke wouldn't work.

In other news, which is only incidentally related (really!), did you hear about the Reuters poll that discovered most women would give up sex for 15 months in exchange for a new wardrobe? (Two percent actually said they'd abstain for three years!) I wonder if that new wardrobe would be filled with I-just-got-out-of-bed t-shirts and camouflage pants. Somehow, I think not.

Anyhow, tonight I think I'll look my sweet husband in the face, while wearing my sexy glasses, and tell him I'm giving up sex for clothes. Then, I'll fill my new wardrobe with lots of coordinating items, no camo, and a hefty amount of things that must be ironed. Maybe my gynecologist (a man) will accept that as a suitable method of birth control.

Married Life:

IT SEEMED LIKE IT WOULD BE FUN.

Does Anyone Care What The Groom Wears?

Recently, a reader submitted a question that reminded me of a common dilemma surrounding military weddings. "Busy Bride" in San Diego asks, "My fiancée will be wearing his dress whites for our wedding, but my gown is actually candlelight white. Will we clash? Will candlelight white and white-white look tacky together?"

Before I answer this, let me define "Candlelight White" for the male readers out there. All your life, you thought you'd marry a girl in white. Now you hear your bride arguing with her mother about the merits of "eggshell" shoes and the camouflaging effect of "linen" nylons. You're not even sure what nylons are, but now you're completely flummoxed that they might come in an assortment of colors, one of them being named after the thing your mother used to put on the kitchen table.

You're probably confused by your bride's new lingo—having already spent several weeks with your fiancée shaking her head at you in disgust because you foolishly suggested that an Xbox 360 be listed on your wedding registry—and you're not about to take any chances guessing what "Candlelight White" might mean. Therefore, my best suggestion is to spend several afternoons at your local paint store, because that's how long it will take to learn and know all the possible shades of white. Yes, there are shades of white. Lucky for you, these shades are more memorable thanks to nifty names like "Oyster," "Igloo," "Marshmallow," and even, "White Duck." These names are probably the paint industry's way of helping men. If you can't guess that "Marshmallow" and "White Duck" are shades of white, you need more help than I can possibly give here.

I'm Just Saying...

Of course, the color of your bride's wedding dress will not be called marshmallow, and I strongly discourage you from using this name in any sentence that also contains "wedding," "dress," "bride," or "nylons." Just to be safe, don't use the word marshmallow in conjunction with anything involving your fiancée. Actually, maybe you'd better just forget the word marshmallow altogether.

The color of your bride's wedding dress will most likely be named after something that brings to mind delicacy: "China," "Antique," "Ivory," "Bone" (think collar bone, ankle bone, or the bone of a petite bird; do not think dog bone) and Candlelight. Whatever you do, don't call the dress white, unless you want to remind her of the Xbox 360-coveting man that you are.

At this point, you might wonder with increasing anxiety how to describe the color of your uniform. If her clothes have fancy color names, yours must, too, right?

Now, go get a pen and paper because you'll want to write down this very important information. Whatever you do, and no matter what you say, it is crucial, for the sake of a happy wedding, and possibly a happy marriage, that you never forget the color of your uniform, which is white. Yes, white. Your type of white doesn't have a special name, which is a subliminal way of reminding you of your virtually unimportant role as the groom. At this point, the ceremony could actually take place without you, so long as the flowers match the bridesmaids' shoes and the bride's earrings compliment the buttons on her dress. To be perfectly honest, when it comes to your attire, no one would even care if you wore the same suit you wore to your high school graduation, because no one, except maybe your own mother, will be looking at you on your wedding day. The photographer will take dozens of pictures of you with your groomsmen, and you might, for a brief second, think this elevates you to the importance of the bride and her bridesmaids. But you will soon learn when it is time to choose photographs for the wedding album that the first pictures to be eliminated from consideration will be any that (1) include your goofy friends, and (2) don't include the bride.

So to review, her dress will look white, but it will be called something else, something feminine and delicate. Your uniform will look white, and it is white, but that is absolutely unimportant and beside the point.

Which, by the way, to get back to the original reader's question, is exactly what I'd tell the bride.

Together We Can Find Some Couples Friends

When you're single, you date individuals. When you're married, you date couples. No, not in that way. What I mean is, your husband may have friends of his own, and you have yours, but sometimes it's nice to have another husband and wife with whom you both get along. Meeting these husband-and-wife pairs can be challenging, especially for military families who move often, and the process isn't unlike the ritual of traditional dating.

Like romantic relationships, budding friendships (even between couples) are delicate. One false move (for example, showing off your T-Rex impression too early) and you're as finished as the man who wears a singing tie on a first date with a woman.

Therefore, when a couple meets another couple with whom they'd like to be friends, standard dating rules should always apply: relationships from the past are best left in the past; annoying habits and bad manners belong at home; and there is (or should be) a three "date" minimum before moving from pleasant small talk to "my step-mother is a witch, and I have six toes." You didn't subject your romantic dates to a rundown of all your past medical procedures and prescription medicines; theoretically, you should give the nice new neighbors the same courtesy.

On some levels, Dustin and I are an excellent team when it comes to meeting new friends. I'd rather slam my toe in a door than make small talk, but Dustin can discuss weather and sports with the best of them. He compensates for my shortcomings and vice versa. In other words, Dustin makes the good first impression, if you will, and then I move forward with what really matters: "When I think about the months of the year, I picture a backwards clock. How about you?"

However, there are times when Dustin and I are out of sync and we bungle the whole get-to-know-you phase, a critical period in any new relationship. At these times, our conversation on the way home from a night out with new friends might go something like this:

DUSTIN: "I think that went pretty well; how about you?"

SARAH: "Yes, except you totally blew it when you mentioned that you don't like cats. I think they are cat people. Cat people never bond with cat haters."

DUSTIN: "And you ordered two drinks. They didn't seem like drinkers."

SARAH: "So! You told them we like Scrabble! Way to reel them in, Dustin!"

DUSTIN: "Ah, well. Guess they won't call us again."

SARAH: "No, probably not."

DUSTIN: "At least the Joneses still like us."

Other times, we are so out of sync, it's a wonder anyone is friends with us at all. Once we had a couple over for dinner and when the conversation went stale, I decided (why, I will never know) to pull out my "Mr. Chin" performance, a party trick that involves painting an upside down face on my chin, hanging over the side of a couch and singing "New York, New York" with a paper towel wrapped around my head. Looking absolutely horrified that I had introduced our new friends to Mr. Chin so soon in the relationship, Dustin stood in the corner giving me the aviation hand signal to "wave off" or "avert."

When I told a couple of old, Chin-worthy friends about this, one sighed and said, "Oh, Sarah, you were trying to force feelings that weren't there. You sped up the friendship too fast." Suddenly my mind went back to pre-marriage days, when it was important not to call a prospective date before he called you, and when you saved goofy things like Mr. Chin for a time when you were sure that your date really really liked you (or, ideally, once he had professed love for you).

I can't proclaim to have been good at this dating stuff when I was on my own, but neither was Dustin. So in that way, I suppose we deserve each other. But together, we are a great couple who I think anyone would want to have dinner with. That is, until they meet my little friend Mr. Chin.

Perfection Is In
The Eye Of The Beholder

Before I tell you how my husband Dustin's head grew as large as a parade float last week at a wedding, I need to tell you about the man getting married. John is a friend from our first sea-going squadron, where intense friendships are historically forged between new members. It's a process similar to strangers being stuck in an elevator and then exiting lifelong friends.

I first met John at an unofficial party with other spouses. John was the newest member of the squadron. Our husbands had already met John at work, so before John arrived, the other wives and I asked for details.

"Is he married?"

"No."

"Darn. Well, is he fun?"

"He doesn't drink," they said. "Like, never. He has never had a drink, ever."

Then, glancing at us and sizing up the atmosphere, one of the guys said, "and he knows every show tune."

The room suddenly grew quiet, after what seemed like a record player coming to a scratching halt. A Navy pilot who has never tasted alcohol and knows all the Broadway songs? They couldn't be serious. Sure, we were stereotyping, but so far, our definition of a Navy pilot was our husbands: loud, sometimes obnoxious, beer-loving guys who would choose NASCAR over Broadway. I'm not saying every Navy pilot is like this—just our husbands. John, therefore, was an anomaly.

I bonded with John instantly. While my husband shared inside jokes with the other guys, John talked to me about movies and music. John was the clown at my son's birthday party. (Yes, my husband has been a clown, too, but never intentionally.) And, get this, John knows how to swing dance.

But John never had a serious woman in his life, and that concerned me. A guy like John should be married, I thought. Then, a few years later, John introduced us to Margaret. I called my Spouse Club friends, who by this time were already scattered across the country, and told them the great news. John had finally found the right girl (she swing dances, too).

So Dustin was a swordsman at John and Margaret's wedding last weekend, and at Margaret's request, Dustin was the one who smacked her in the rear with his sword and called out, "Welcome to the Navy." You see, Margaret has a special affection for my husband and thinks that he must be "perfect." Margaret has never lived with Dustin.

Later, at the reception, I was standing alone, feeling uncomfortable in my postpartum-body and clothes that don't fit, when a group of young girls beside me started whispering. They were wearing dresses with thin spaghetti straps, which after having three children and nursing two, I'll never wear again. Their made-up faces were smooth and had no creases around the eyes. They had long legs and high heels. And, on second glance, I realized they were staring at my husband on the other side of the room in his spiffy Navy uniform. The giggling girls ran over to have their pictures taken with Dustin. They hung on him and posed. They laughed like school children. And although Dustin's face was red with embarrassment, I knew his head was inflating to irreversible proportions.

The gaggle of girls ran back to their places near me and formed a huddle.

"He's so hot," one of them said.

"You should go talk to him," her friends encouraged. "I haven't seen him with anyone."

I laughed and the girls looked over, their smiles turning to shock. "Is that your husband?" they asked.

I nodded.

The girls had been fooled by Dustin's uniform. It's a hazard as old as the military. Women see a man in uniform, and it doesn't matter who he really is, the women already have an idea that he is "hot" like Tom Cruise in "Top Gun," or a romantic like Richard Gere in "An Officer and a Gentleman." Uniforms make all service members look identically handsome and refined. But it's just an illusion. Just ask their wives. For beneath those well-pressed jackets and shiny shoes, Navy men are as different as, well, as different as Dustin and John. And perfection truly is in the eyes of the beholder ... so long as that "beholder" doesn't live with you.

Online Banking Ruined Shopping

Some hail the inception of email and the Internet into military life as the best thing since microwavable macaroni-and-cheese. Others know that nothing comes without cost, and there is a bitter tradeoff for having your loved one wired to the Web while they are out at sea.

There once was a time when "deployment widows" could take advantage of time alone by shopping and redecorating. When Dustin is away, I ease the loneliness with my old friends—Pottery Barn and Target. You see, Dustin has a problem with money. Mainly, he won't part with it. Ever. He still lives in a place (his mind) where a woman's dress should cost $10.00 and a pregnant mother should only have one or two maternity outfits.

Once, after returning from deployment, Dustin was absolutely stunned that I had purchased a new pair of shoes during the six months that he was away. "You bought a new pair of shoes?" he said. "Why did you need a new pair of shoes?" I decided not to tell him about all the clothes, makeup and baby toys I had also purchased.

What's worse, Dustin has a strong opinion about everything he won't spend money on. He has tried to talk me out of nearly every purchase by exercising his "right" to have a violent and profound negative reaction to it.

"I can't believe you'd actually want to sleep under a RED quilt," he once said. "Who could possibly feel restful under all that red?"

Never mind this is the man who would sleep on a bare mattress and not turn on the heat in the dead of winter just to save a buck, but apparently Dustin has particularities when it comes to which color he will or will not sleep under.

Basically, every purchase we make, right down to toilet paper and toothbrushes, has the potential to become an argument. To save our marriage, I delay all my "needless" (Dustin's words) splurges for times when Dustin is safely in another state or country. All the better if he is deployed on a giant gray ship, in the middle of the Atlantic Ocean.

And then the Navy got email.

I thought my heart had stopped the first time Dustin sent me an email message from deployment asking, "Why did you spend $50 at Target today?"

How did he know that? I was ready to point fingers at my partners in crime (friends from the Spouse Club) for snitching to their husbands. Then Dustin wrote again: "Why did you take money out of the savings account last night?"

I stared at the computer screen in horror as I realized my newest foe: online banking.

Dustin claims he once tried to balance the checkbook via the Internet, and each time he refreshed the screen a new debit appeared at the top of the list. I was spending money right before his eyes, and I didn't even know I'd been caught. My deployment shopping days were over.

Several months later, once Dustin was again on dry land but busy with his laptop in the other room, I decided to sell some stuff on eBay. What I wanted was a new mirror that Dustin wouldn't buy, so I set my mind on making money on eBay to buy it myself. Except each time a bidder put money into our online payment account that night, a handful of money was taken out. What is going on? I thought, scratching my head. Then I realized that while I was auctioning off old clothes and making money, Dustin was in the next room bidding on baseball cards. As fast I was making money, he was spending it.

I called out to Dustin in a huff. "I'm working my tail off to make us some money, and you're spending it right out from under me!"

Dustin laughed. "Welcome to my world every single day," he said.

Shopping will never be the same again.

Squeaky Wheel Gets The Better Table

If Dustin had his way, he'd go through life unnoticed. His motto: "Stay neutral and never make a scene." Dustin is a mediator. A diplomat. The one who makes peace with everyone, in every situation.

All of which makes him well-suited for the military lifestyle, but incredibly difficult to live with.

For example, last month, while we were in Virginia visiting family, we went out for a nice dinner with seven adults and two children. Incidentally, it was prom night. Need I say more? It's not easy to stay incognito with a group that consists of two children and my father-in-law ... on prom night.

At the hostess stand, Dustin's face showed his discomfort. He stared at the ground, positioned himself in the corner, and acted like he didn't know Ford, 5, and Owen, 3, when they sang "I like to move it, move it," from the movie "Madagascar."

Our wait time was estimated to be an hour and a half, unless of course we were willing to sit outside, where it was forecasted (by the hostess) to be "somewhat chilly." Then our wait time was only five minutes.

"We'll sit outside," said my older, impatient brother, Van, who was incidentally the only one in our group dressed in jeans and long sleeves.

All nine of us snaked our way between tables filled with teenagers in updo's and revealing sequined dresses until we had reached our cold metal table outside.

"It's freezing out here," my mom said.

"I'm cold," said Owen.

"Even the chair hurts," said Ford.

Dustin sat at the end of the table, chattering his teeth behind blue lips, not daring to make a fuss or complain.

Mother's intuition told me that waiting longer than about two minutes for a table inside was out of the question, but I was looking at a group of chilly, miserable diners. So when the waiter came to take our order, I said (much louder than I had intended), "Could you bring us some white table cloths to use as blankets?" The moment the words escaped my lips, I looked at Dustin and could see that he was horrified. He'd rather die frozen to the metal chair than wrap himself in a white tablecloth at a public restaurant. There were people walking by on the sidewalk, for crying out loud!

"Of course I'll bring you some tablecloths," the apologetic waiter said. "How many do you need?"

"Just bring a handful," I said, but I knew we'd only use eight—one for each person, minus Dustin.

When the waiter left, Dustin looked at me and said, "Are you really going to wrap yourself in a tablecloth?"

"Don't you know me at all?" I said. "Of course I'm going to wrap up in a tablecloth." (Secretly, I was planning to wear it like a cape and tell the boys that I was Superwoman.)

Just when I thought Dustin was ready to divorce me, however, a man with a blue shirt and red tie came out to our table. His name tag had MANAGER on it.

"Remember that long wait my hostess quoted you?" he said. "It just got a lot shorter. How does one minute sound? We have a table ready for you inside."

My family leapt to their feet.

"What luck," they said. "Today must be our lucky day!"

I wasn't buying it. How did our wait time go from 90 minutes to one minute? Why were we suddenly thrust to the front of the long line streaming outside of the restaurant?

Then it occurred to me. When the manager saw the waiter gathering tablecloths for the diners outside to use as blankets—while prospective patrons walked by the very nice restaurant on the sidewalk—well, we emerged as accidental VIPs. The manager wasn't extending an olive branch. He was saving face.

I'm Just Saying...

"A table full of people draped in robes like 'ET' isn't good for business, eh?" I said as I walked by the manager on my way to the warm table inside. He just smiled.

Once we were inside enjoying our bread and stripping hot layers from our wardrobe, Dustin looked over the table at me and winked. I suppose he had finally realized that the old saying is true. Sometimes the squeaky wheel does get a better table.

How Husbands Get Their Nicknames

There's one thing smart military wives (and I'm not claiming to be one of them) learn quickly. In the presence of your husband's co-workers (members of his squadron, unit, etc.) it's never a good idea to reveal any embarrassing facts about his habits, his childhood, or his favorite reality TV show.

Unfortunate slip-ups such as these usually result in even more unfortunate nicknames (or "call signs" for you pilots), with the worst consequence of all being that the guilty wife's name will always be attached to the story (told over and over and over again) about how her husband earned his dreadful nickname.

I once knew a wife who sent her deployed husband a package addressed to "Honey Bear." He was instantly nicknamed, and the new call sign was applied to his flight suit.

Another wife sent pictures of the couple's cats with "We miss you Daddy" printed at the top. Her husband may have called the kitties "Pooky" and "Tinkerbell" and loved on them like children in the privacy of his own home, but I'm sure the public broadcast of his feline fancies was a bit unexpected and embarrassing.

I also knew a girl who sent her husband's squadron a picture of him from the 5th grade, when he was sporting buckteeth and a devastating brown flannel shirt.

Oh, wait, that was me.

It's hard for us women to understand why telling "The Guys" that your husband tapes every episode of "Survivor" (or worse, "JAG") can be so humiliating, but maybe the embarrassment is equivalent to what I would feel if my husband told everyone what I look like at 7 o'clock in the morning or that I sat on a table when I was eight-months pregnant and broke it.

We can't really be blamed for our unintentional slip-ups. Sometimes we don't even see the potential humor of a secret we are about to disclose. For instance, Dustin is often told that he looks like Tom Cruise. At a Navy dinner party, I told the group that I think he looks more like Dustin Hoffman. How was I to know that "Rain Man" and "Tootsie" would be the new names tossed around in consideration for his call sign?

"But what about 'The Graduate'?" I said. "I meant that you look like Dustin Hoffman in 'The Graduate'."

"You don't understand," Dustin said. "Why would they call me 'The Graduate' when 'Tootsie' is so humiliating?"

This need to exploit your buddies until their faces turn red must be a guy thing. I couldn't imagine my friends saying to me, "Wow, you got so big when you were pregnant, you snapped that table right in half!" Or, "Without your makeup, Sarah, you look a lot like Marge Simpson." This contributes to our innocence when it comes to exposing our husbands' quirks and embarrassing favorites. It makes no sense to us that friends would manipulate such personal knowledge.

So when I say that my husband sings like a howling dog or that his mommy kept his childhood bunk beds until he was twenty-eight years old, I really mean no harm, and I am oblivious to the consequences it may cause him at work with his buddies. After all, he's my little Dusty-Wusty. Why would I want to embarrass him?

I'm Just Saying…

CHILDREN

Being Mom:

SOMEDAY I WILL HAVE A VERY SMALL PURSE.

The Amish Are Coming!

A few weeks ago, a friend knocked on my door and handed me a plastic kitchen bag filled with goo. Attached to the bag was a sheet of paper with "Amish Friendship Bread" printed on it.

"You just feed this batter and then cook it to make bread," the friend said.

It sounded easy enough, and with a name like "Amish Friendship Bread," how could it be anything but amiable?

For the first few days, the goo-filled bag sat innocently enough on my kitchen counter. The beige batter in the bottom filled only about one-eighth of the bag. I wondered how such a tiny amount of batter would ever make two loaves of bread, plus four more bags of goo, as the instructions said it would.

On the fourth day, I added milk, sugar and flour to the mix.

"Are you sure I still leave this thing out on the counter?" I asked my friend. "Even though it has milk in it now?"

"Yep," she said, a tinge of delight in her voice, as if she was keeping a secret, like waiting for me to sit on a whoopee cushion.

The day after I added milk, sugar and flour, and continued to leave the bag on the kitchen counter (despite my better judgment and my mother's voice in my head telling me to always put the milk back in the refrigerator), I woke to the smell of beer. Fermented beer. In the kitchen, the goo was growing. The plastic bag was so full of air, it looked pregnant. Overnight, the batter had doubled in size. Or, if you'd rather, it had procreated.

"It's like a beast," I said out loud, and my children began to look scared.

"Stop feeding it," Owen, 5, said.

"We don't really need bread, do we?" asked Ford, 7.

I let air out of the bag, releasing a yeasty smell at the same time, and reassured the children that the batter would not take over our house, even though I wasn't entirely sure of that myself. I was beginning to see how the "beast" would eventually make two loaves of bread and four extra bags of beastlings.

The instructions warned that after making the bread, if you failed to keep a beastling for yourself, you would have to wait for a friend to give one back to you, because "only the Amish know how to make the starter." This seemed like a vague threat to me. The beast—I mean, batter—had been passed down from neighbor to neighbor for hundreds of years. If I broke the chain, I feared that something awful—something like receiving the Amish Unfriendly Bread next time—would happen.

By the end of the week, I found myself very afraid of the growing batter on my kitchen counter. I eyed it when I walked into the room, and I never turned my back on it. Like a dragon curled up next to my coffee pot, the bag spit out air, hissed, and made bad smells.

I wasn't sure I wanted to make bread with it.

Finally the day came when I could unleash the beast and add normal things like eggs, vanilla, and cinnamon to it, which I had hoped would mask the smell. When I was done baking, I had two surprisingly delicious loaves of bread and four bags of beastlings to disperse. It occurred to me then that if the Amish ever wanted to kill off an entire species of non-Amish people slowly over time, they could probably do it with this never-ending bread that people willingly—gleefully, even—pass on to their neighbors, four at a time.

Dustin took the extra bags of batter and one loaf of bread to work and dared people to take it home to their wives. I suspect it was one of the first (and last) times something Amish came onto a Navy base. If the batter could speak, which over time it may learn to do, I think it would have protested and called itself a Conscientious Objector.

Kathy, who works in the same office with Dustin, was up for the challenge and took a beastling home. Over the next week, I received several panicked calls from her. "Are you sure I leave it on the counter? Will it explode? Is it supposed to smell like this?"

The cycle had continued, as the Amish have intended it to do for hundreds of years.

Yesterday I got another call from Kathy. She had made the bread, produced four beastlings, and sent one to her military-spouse daughter in North Carolina, who like so many before her, was afraid at first, but carried on and made the bread anyway. She sent a loaf to her husband in Afghanistan and passed four bags of goo on to her military-spouse friends.

Which is to say, the batter continues to grow and reproduce, and now it has infiltrated the military. Don't open your door; you could be next.

If Only You Had Retrieved My Clown Nose

Every store I go to these days seems to have a special "discount card." Sometimes it is called a "super savings card" or a "valued customer membership," but always it means that ultimately the store wants your personal information so that they can harass you during dinner.

I'm opposed to these cards for several reasons, one of the biggest being that I'm a military wife. I don't have enough time in one city to collect discount cards. My wallet is already filled with credit cards and driver's licenses, all invalid and with various old addresses on them. I still have a library card from San Diego, Calif. I haven't lived in California in five years.

What's more, by the time these companies process my information, which I suspect somehow includes my phone number, address, and blood type, and they begin contacting me, my family has already moved. A grocery store in Jacksonville, Fla., still sends me coupon flyers that are forwarded from my previous address to my new one. I can't handle any more stores stalking me this way.

But I'm also opposed to these cards because basically my brain becomes mush inside a store. It's all part of my DNA as a woman. It's the same part that causes me to pause and take a deep breath in front of a shoe display and renders me helpless at Target. "What on earth did I come here for?" I say walking up and down the aisles like a zombie. In that moment, I am no longer in control. Instead of going "straight to the paper towels" as planned, I wander through the children's clothing, appliances and books. When I get to the checkout counter with a mound of things I didn't need in my cart, I feel like someone waking up from a dream: "Where am I? Why am I here?" So when the salesperson says, "Would you like to apply for a card and get ten percent off today?" I usually just look at her and go, "Huh?"

See, these stores are entirely set up to make people spend money. They have sales meetings designed to accomplish that very task. Marketing people study our habits and make reports on them. There are books written about it and strategies devised to make us spend more and more money. So is it any wonder that we are thrown off guard when asked to apply for a "savings card"? (*Savings what? But I thought I was here to spend money!*)

Yesterday I was at an office supply store, my hands full of new pens, highlighters and other things I didn't need, when a sales person asked "Have you signed up for our savings card?"

I looked at her and dropped my purchases on the counter. I opened my purse, and thanks to someone (ahem, Owen) trying to help me "organize" the day before, my wallet looked like it had vomited inside my bag. Credit cards and loose change spilled out like rice from a Chinese takeout box. I had to flip through grocery store "VIP" cards from Jacksonville and San Diego to find my debit card. And then, Ford's red foam clown nose (I'm not kidding) bounced out of my purse, across the counter and onto the floor.

I looked at the salesperson and wanted to say, "Do I look like someone who has time to fill out an application? Do I look like I need any more cards? Does it look like I'll be happy to hear from you when your company calls during dinner eight months from now?"

But the expression on the salesperson's face told me that my sentiments needn't even be said. She rang up my purchases in silence.

Back in my car, I felt angry about the whole thing. Instead of helping me fetch Ford's clown nose, the salesperson stood there and gawked, all the while gripping that application like precious gold. Plus, my pants were too tight. (It was that kind of day.)

So, I marched back into the store, prepared to tell the sales person this: "I don't want to be on any lists, so stop asking me every time I come in here!" Yet, as soon as the sliding doors opened and the smell of vinyl notebook binders came over me, I found myself instead wandering up and down the aisles, scratching my head and muttering, "Where am I, and why am I here?"

Some Things Parents Don't Need

Being a seasoned mother of young children teaches you things. Most of these things are in direct opposition to what catalogs selling toys and baby gear would have you believe. For instance, a recent perusal of the various catalogs that arrived in my mailbox yesterday—a stack that stands taller than a small dog—shows me that some people would like me to think that my 9-month-old son Lindell's happy childhood memories are at stake if his bottom is not cleaned with wipes warmed in a machine first. His pacifier will make him sick if it isn't sprayed with a special (expensive), non-toxic cleaner. They would also like me to believe that toddlers need a leash to go out in public.

Six years ago, when Ford was a baby, I fell victim to these ploys. I am embarrassed to admit that I spent an inordinate amount of time researching strollers, finally settling on one so expensive, excessive, and unnecessary that my husband, being the safety-conscious military pilot that he is, asked, "Does it come with airbags?"

Me: "Do you think strollers need them? The catalog didn't show any with airbags. Maybe I should look again."

Dustin: "No, but at that price, it better come with something."

Two kids later, I've learned that not only are airbags on strollers not necessary, so are most other things, including padding. Lindell's favorite ride is a cheap umbrella stroller that he sits in like he is lounging in a hammock.

Here is a list of other superfluous items I found in yesterday's collection of catalogs.

Inflatable Sled with Three-Sided Enclosure

Something tells me this isn't what little Johnny had in mind when he asked for a sled. If you haven't seen one of these new, safer sleds, picture Disney World's spinning teacups made entirely out of an inflatable raft. There is zero chance that a child on one of these sleds will enjoy any of childhood's simple pleasures, such as going headfirst off the wooden Radio Flyer and straight into a pile of snow.

It's snow! I can't think of anything else that provides a safer landing, except for maybe a pile of bubble wrap, and as of yet, I haven't seen any for sale in my catalogs.

Locking Storage for Household Cleaning Supplies

This is actually a very good idea and a great safety item. After three kids, however, I've learned that I don't clean nearly as much as I thought I did.

Wireless Child Locator

This friendly looking bear clips to your child's shoe and the receiver stays with you (by they way, your toddler should also stay with you). At the push of a button, a "high-decibel beep" alerts you to your child's location, up to 150-feet away, "even through concrete walls."

There is an easier and less expensive way to keep your children from wandering off. It involves a pocketful of Tootsie Pops and some very stern warnings, or "threats" if you'd prefer. But if losing your children on the other side of a concrete wall is a problem, there is always the child leash [shudder].

Plastic Seat Protector

This sturdy sheet of plastic goes over your finer furniture to protect it from leaky diapers and hands sticky with apple juice. This is only useful, however, if you have already ignored other people's advice to not have nice furniture until your children are in college.

Plastic Car Seat Protector

A second cousin of the Plastic Seat Protector, this item goes beneath your child's car seat to spare your upholstery the damage that befalls most things in close proximity to a toddler. You can wrap your entire backseat in plastic if you want, but your child will still get ketchup on the ceiling.

Mosquito Netting for Stroller

This net that goes on the front of a stroller protects your child from dangerous, oncoming insects. Really, though, how fast are these parents walking that bugs are pelting their children at high speeds? Then again, I do live in Florida, where love bug season can turn the front of a white car black, and I suppose, no one wants to come back from a family walk to find their child with bugs in their teeth.

But be careful because it's a slippery slope: first the netting, then the airbag.

Summer Trip
Makes Me Want A Gun

I grew up in Virginia Beach, Va., which meant that my parents had easy access to all kinds of educational day trips. This wasn't always a good thing. For me, at least. Trips to Colonial Williamsburg, Jamestown, and Monticello were all learning experiences unsuccessfully wrapped up in what was supposed to look like "fun." I wasn't buying it.

So it came as a surprise (to myself, mostly, but I can only guess it was to my parents as well) when I decided during a recent trip to my parents' house (now in Smithfield, Va.) that I should take my 6- and 4-year old sons to Colonial Williamsburg … just for the fun of it. I even said, "It will be fun and educational."

Initially, I worried that my boys were too young to understand the Revolutionary War and Colonial Virginians. Then, once we were there and watching 21st century men and women dressed up in hoop skirts, collars, and white wigs, pretending with full conviction that they are 18th century men and women having fun (laughing in the streets with their colonial neighbors; dancing in the palace; riding on horses that relieve themselves at the feet of paying customers) and feeling all revolutionary, I worried that my boys just wouldn't get it. The educational part, that is. They definitely understood what the horses were doing, and for them, it was hilarious.

Then we passed a quaint little shop with a woman crocheting innocently enough while rocking in a chair on the front porch. She seemed so friendly, so inviting. But she was only a façade. Inside her little shop filled with 18th century things (like disposable cameras) was a train wreck waiting to happen. My boys wanted guns. They wanted big, long wooden things the salesperson called "muskets," possibly because she thought that might confuse me into believing I wasn't really buying weapons for my young children. Not only that, but these muskets were expensive. Ford wanted the realistic one that made a popping sound. Owen wanted the unadorned wooden one that looked like something his father could have made ... for free. Both boys' selections, however, were equally expensive.

Now, before I tell you that within 15 minutes of being in the store I told young Owen, "Please at least get the expensive gun that looks real," I need to tell you about the general atmosphere of the place. Basically, it was the size of a glorified closet with lots of high-priced merchandise stacked on the tables and spilling onto the floors. There were children everywhere begging their moms for muskets and triangle felt hats to which their fathers would surely object. Everyone was having a temper tantrum. My Owen was the loudest of them all. He wanted the plain, expensive musket, and there was no talking him out of it. Telling him that the more realistic one his brother picked was a better deal was of no use. At the checkout counter, a nice woman in a bonnet took all the cash I had in my wallet and then asked, "Is there anything else we can help you with today?" Because Owen was still having a fit on the floor beside me and Ford was "shooting" passersby, I said, "Yes, where's the closest colonial liquor store?" But she didn't think that was funny.

Off we went to explore more of Williamsburg with two Revolutionary soldiers—guns, triangle hats and all—at our sides. Along the way we met an 18th century man in a white wig who called himself Mr. BB. My precocious Ford, who introduced himself as hailing from the "colony of Florida," had a long talk with Mr. BB, filling him in on what he could expect in the 21st century, if he should live that long: indoor plumbing, DVD players, and President Bush. I was standing alongside them, snapping pictures, beaming with pride, and wearing what I thought was a fashionable empire-waist shirt, when Mr. BB, in his knee-length britches, turned to me and said, "Madame, should you be in this heat in your condition?" (Just so you know, "your condition" is the colonial way of saying "pregnant." And just in case you are confused, no, I am not pregnant.) At this point, I'd had enough of colonial role playing. So, without taking my eyes off Mr. BB, and without responding to his faux pas, I simply said to Ford, out of the corner of my mouth, "OK, that's it; hand me your musket."

I Think I Learned Too Much This Summer

For more weeks than you probably care to know, I've been on the road visiting family. Road trips used to be so easy before I was married and had children, mostly because, well, I didn't make very many road trips back then. Traveling with children could be an Olympic event of sorts. Just transporting all the luggage is hard work. I have three boys, but I'm vacationing with five suitcases, one of them explicitly for toys, swimmies, Batman capes, pirate swords and everything else that must go along with children. Oh, and did I mention that I'm also traveling with my 87-year-old grandmother, Doris? Not surprisingly, she is the easiest one of all. She only carries a fresh pair of pantyhose (to wear with her tennis shoes), a couple of dresses (she's never worn pants), a pocket book, a wool scarf (yes, even in summer), and a plastic bag with her medicine.

Now, I know that it is summer break for my kids, but this trip has been quite educational nonetheless. And I don't just say that because we've visited places like Colonial Williamsburg.

Our first stop was at a NASCAR race in Dover, Del., where we stayed with one of our squadron mate's parents. There I learned that our friend Mr. John, as the kids call him, really does have a Yoda made entirely out of Legos. I also saw pictures of him in the first grade, and he looked just the same as he does now ... like a kid who would make a Yoda entirely out of Legos.

At the NASCAR race, I learned that my 4- and 6-year-old boys know more about racing than I initially thought. I learned that stock cars are very (very!) loud, the drivers are kind of cute, and there is math even in racing (the back of one spectator's car had a sticker on it that read: 8x3=24. And if you know what that means, you've probably watched too many races, too).

Next, we went to my in-law's house in Fairfax, Va. There I learned that fathers and grandfathers are no fun to take to museums because they read every plaque and tend to wander away from the group, causing major confusion and loss of patience. I also learned that when I suggest we take the Metro to the Air and Space Museum and my husband says, "Nah, it's not that far; let's walk," the museum is probably 18 blocks away.

By the way, on the streets of Washington, D.C., I hit a new "low" (depending on how you look at it): I actually breastfed our 5-month-old baby while I walked down the sidewalk. I was covered, yes, by a nifty little contraption called, quite fittingly, a "Hooter Hider," but still, nursing a baby while disciplining my other boys and keeping up with my younger, childless sister-in-law proved very difficult and humiliating. Bystanders at the crosswalks in our nation's capitol graciously pretended not to notice when my baby made slurping and burping noises beneath the "Hooter Hider."

Our next stop was in Smithfield, Va., where the boys and I said goodbye to Dustin (he flew back home to Florida) and stayed with my mom and dad for three weeks. This is where we met up with my brother and his wife, and I learned that Will still likes to keep the car cold enough to hang meat in. Some things never change, like the smell of Mom's antiques, my dad's faded blue jeans, and the way everyone yells "SARAH!" up the stairs if I've slept in too late.

From time to time, I checked in with Dustin back home, and although I worried that he would be lonely without us, he seemed to be having a good time. Friends invited him to dinner and asked if he needed anything (does anyone do this for us when our husbands are gone?). He played golf, watched NASCAR, hung out with Mr. John, and got a lot of work done. My friends checked to see that he was keeping my plants alive and the house relatively clean. I learned that he was.

Now we are nearing the end of our trip, yet I still have one lingering question, one last thing to learn: how exactly did our suitcases and their contents actually multiply while we weren't looking ... and will we be able to get it all home?

A Little Less Antibacterial

I'm doing the best I can to get last night's dishes put away, and if the kids have clean socks, well, I consider that a bonus. But then I'm sitting down to watch television and a commercial comes on for antibacterial window cleaner. *My windows have bacteria on them? I wonder.* And then, *when was the last time I cleaned the windows anyway?*

For a moment I am panicked. I even toy with the idea of getting up to inspect the windows. But no, I sit back down again, totally satisfied that at least I was able to get the gum off the bottom of Owen's shoe today.

One of Dustin's favorite stories is that before he left for his first deployment, I wiped down the surfaces of the nursery prior to going to bed each night. Ford was only four weeks old. He had never even laid on the floor without a blanket, much less mouthed the corners of the dresser. Yet there I was with the wipes, cleaning up dirt that could only have come into the room on the bottom of a spider's leg, because I didn't even let anyone wear shoes inside the house.

When Dustin came home from that deployment just weeks before Ford's first birthday, someone asked him, "What was the hardest thing to get used to after being gone so long?" Dustin's answer: "Instead of boiling the pacifier each time it dropped, Sarah just stuck it in her mouth and sucked off the dirt."

That's the difference the first year of motherhood makes. In the beginning, everything must be scoured clean. But eventually managing such feats as making dinner and ironing shirts becomes life's greatest goal.

When I tell Ford, now almost 5 years old, about "the days when Mom washed everything in the nursery with disinfectant," he laughs so hard that I think he will have an accident. That's because Ford can't imagine his mom—his mom who lets Owen, 2, wear his Superman cape from the dirty clothes—worrying about things like germy windows.

Yet surely Ford and Owen have noticed commercials on television for toys made of antimicrobial substances. Surely, they are aware that some people at least are concerned about microbes. But Ford and Owen don't know any of these people because all our friends are by pure coincidence seasoned parents. Only a brand new mother has the patience to disinfect toys.

And that's exactly what the antibacterial industry is banking on, that mothers' fears of disease-infested molecules landing on their child's crib will actually prompt them to buy a teething ring made with Microban.

So, with the time and emotional distance I now have from the insanity-provoking first year of motherhood—along with my recent and total disinterest in the antibacterial industry—let me help new mothers put things back into perspective.

First, realize that you can't get rid of all the germs. Think about it; some companies are trying to sell you dog toys with antimicrobial protection. Yes, that's right; the same dog who eats his own feces needs to have his chew toy protected with Microban. (On second thought, perhaps it is because of the dog's eating habits that his toy needs protection.) But even if Fido's bone is sanitized, what about the slobbery tennis ball your toddler throws for him?

Second, some things just don't need to be that clean. Are people really licking your windows? Is anyone eating the grout in your bathroom shower?

Third, remember that our bodies are more resilient than we think. During the times that I worried about germs in Ford's nursery, my Navy dad liked to say, "POWs ate roaches to stay alive." Of course, no one wants their child to eat a roach, and no one considers POWs' living conditions acceptable, but Dad's point is clear: We don't give our bodies enough credit.

All this is not to say that people should live like slobs, but we do need to exercise common sense. Until Ford chooses to eat his meals on the ironing board, I simply refuse to worry about the germs there. Until Owen actually puts the dog's tennis ball in his own mouth, I'm not going to worry about that either.

Maybe I'm wrong on this, but I'd rather put my energy towards more important things—like finally folding the laundry and doing last night's dishes.

Appreciating All The Firsts

Our oldest son, Ford, 5, was born the day before Thanksgiving. A few days later, Dustin left on an aircraft carrier. It was our first taste of the Navy's dirty little secret—prior to a six-month deployment, military personnel will spend six months preparing for the event by going on a series of home-again/gone-again training missions, during which time they are home very little.

In that first year, Dustin missed Ford's first smile, first giggle and first steps. He wasn't there to hold him after his shots or to see him taste solid food. Dustin literally watched our son grow from an infant to a toddler via digital pictures. By the time Dustin returned, just a few weeks shy of Ford's first birthday, our son didn't really know who "Dad" was.

This, by the way, is something military families rarely get over. The sting of so many missed "firsts" is not easily soothed. You can't get those months—those moments—back. But life goes on, and soldiers return, which leads to the other dirty little secret of military life: While you once vowed never to take family time for granted, before long, life becomes routine again, and you hardly take notice that your husband was home for baby's first "time out."

Fast-forward to a quiet Sunday last month. It began as an ordinary day in a non-deployment year. I had shooed my family out the door so that I could have time to myself and maybe get some laundry done. Dustin, Ford and our youngest son, Owen, were outside on the driveway. I was in the living room folding pajamas. Suddenly, I heard a commotion coming from the garage. Something—I don't know, perhaps my Mother Radar—made me investigate.

The first thing I noticed when I walked into the garage was the training wheels from Ford's bike scattered across the cement floor.

Then I heard the clank of metal tools hitting the driveway. When I rounded the corner, I saw my boys hovering over Ford's bike, which now had only two wheels. Before I knew it, my firstborn was teetering atop a big-boy bike in the front lawn, with his dad running behind, desperately holding on to the back of the seat.

I could barely watch.

Next, to my horror, Ford and Dustin moved from the safety of the grass to the pavement of the street. Over and over again, I witnessed my son falling off his bike and slamming into the curb. First, it was his chin skimming across the pavement. Then, it was his knee. Bam! Time and time again, Ford came to a crashing halt ... flat on the street.

He had learned how to ride, now he needed to learn how to stop.

Distressed and anxious, I went back inside to fold laundry. As I picked up each of Ford's size 5T pants, I marveled at how it seems like just yesterday that I sent Dustin an email on the ship announcing, "Ford can sit up and clap his hands!"

I occasionally peeked out the window to see how things were going on the street. It was like watching surgery on television. Through the veil of fingers, I dared myself to watch Ford "ride" his bike, knowing full well the image of him falling would haunt me forever.

Just before dinner time, Dustin ran into the house and said, "Quick, come look!"

I threw down my oven mitt and followed Dustin to the driveway. There we held hands and smiled as we watched Ford confidently riding—and stopping—his bike ... all by himself.

I will never forget the firsts that Dustin missed—Ford's first smile, his first word, his first steps—but I hope, for the rest of my days, I will always remember that for all those missed moments, Dustin was home for many more. And that makes those memories all the more special.

Red Cape, Blue Tights Are Boy's Rite Of Passage

Just when I'd finally learned everything I need to know about Matchbox cars, my son, Ford, the one who's goal seemingly used to be to own more small metal cars than anyone else in the world, is now on to something else: Superman.

"But, Ford," I said, "Mom just figured out how to put this complicated race track together. Don't you want to play with your Matchbox cars anymore?"

I only have myself to blame for this. I'm the one who bought the Superman video that is now Ford's object of affection. Selfishly, I thought the superhero flick might relieve me of hearing the "Blue's Clues" theme song one more time. I didn't realize it would thrust us into a whole new boyhood rite-of-passage.

Suddenly, the living room is littered with Superman books and figurines, and the hundreds of Matchbox cars we've collected over the last year are only used as "big, heavy objects" for the Man of Steel to lift.

I resisted this transition at first. Silly me, I thought "Blue's Clues" was getting annoying. I didn't realize that abandoning it would mean the end of my son's babyhood and the beginnings of a "little boy" who likes super heroes, plays pretend-wrestle, and [wincing] thinks anyone with a red cape on their back can fly.

But Superman has been living at our house for quite some time now, so last week I figured that I should join the frenzy and learn what makes this man in blue tights so interesting. Despite having two older brothers, I managed to remain a girly-girl who loved Barbie and makeup. I really had a lot to figure out when it comes to Superman.

One night at dinner, I asked my son and husband some questions. "So, Lois Lane doesn't know that Clark Kent is Superman, right?"

"Right," they said, laughing at my ignorance.

"And Lois Lane thinks Clark Kent is really cute, right?"

"No, no, no. Lois thinks Clark is goofy. She likes Superman. Clark just works with her at the newspaper."

"Ah," I said. "Well, Ford, that's pretty cool that Lois writes for a newspaper ... just like Mommy!"

"I guess so," he shrugged.

Mom isn't as interesting as she used to be either (another casualty of the transition from baby to boy)—even if she does share some traits with Lois.

Ford then turned to his dad (with great excitement, I might add) and the two talked superhero-talk for the rest of our meal.

I tuned out, retreating to the places in my mind where Ford is still a baby and likes to watch "Baby Mozart." If only I had appreciated the priceless situation of having the little boy all to myself when his daddy was away, when without interference, I could teach Ford how to play the piano, take him to "Blue's Clues Live," and tell him that things like wrestling and play-fighting are too rough for indoors.

But my interest in the conversation between my son and husband piqued again when I heard my name. Dustin was explaining to Ford the history between Lois and Clark/Superman.

"You see, Lois thinks Clark is a nerd and really boring," Dustin said. "But she loves Superman because he is strong, fast, smart and good looking. Lois doesn't realize that Superman *is* Clark Kent. It's the same way your mom thinks that I'm just 'Dustin,' but when she's not looking, I turn into the sexiest man alive."

OK, so maybe I can get into this Superman thing after all. Apparently, there are some great lessons to be learned from the superhero in blue tights: no man is what he seems, women love a man's potential, and all men think they can be Superman, because the women in their lives—beginning with their mother—let them believe it.

My Superman
Is Afraid Of The Dark

A few weeks ago, I wrote about my son Ford's fascination with Superman, and I received dozens of responses from readers. It seems that anyone who's ever had a boy can relate to the trials and tribulations of raising a superhero.

While the Man of Steel is still King of the Toy Chest here at the Smiley house, and I still mourn the absence of "Blue's Clues," I'm beginning to take another look at this boyhood rite of passage.

Ford has now progressed from wanting to play make-believe Superman to believing that he IS Superman. And his younger brother, Owen, who at 15 months old weighs in at a mere 17 pounds and hasn't yet begun to walk, has been given the title of Flash, the Fastest Man Alive and Superman's partner in saving the world. I can't help but laugh as I watch them play together. Picture Ford dressed in full Superman gear, running around the house with his arms outstretched and humming the movie's theme song. About a minute after Ford dashes past me on his mission to save the dog from some evil nemesis, Flash comes crawling by with his binkie and blankey in tow.

Sometimes I worry that Ford has taken this fascination a little too far, especially when he insists on wearing the red cape to restaurants and demands that everyone call him Superman.

Of course, my concern has not prevented me from cleverly parlaying this game into a teaching tool, or a way to get some help around the house: "Superman! Hurry, I need someone to put these Legos back in the toy basket!" "Quick, Superman! Flash dropped his bottle. Can you go save the day and pick it up?"

Today, however, as I walked through the mall with my pint-sized superhero running beside me yelling, "I'm off to save the world," I began to worry. Saving the whole world? That's quite a responsibility for a 3-year-old.

In the car on the way home, I talked to Ford about understanding the difference between make-believe and reality. "For instance, Ford" I said, "you realize Owen isn't really the Fastest Man Alive, right? It's just fun to call him Flash and pretend."

"Right, Mom" he said. "Owen's not really Flash, but I AM Superman!"

"Well Ford, do you understand that even Superman isn't perfect and that he had lots of people who helped him, like his mom and dad?"

"No, Mom, nothing hurts Superman, and he's not afraid of anything. Well, except for coconut [how Ford says kryptonite]."

Ten minutes later, when I pulled into the driveway, Ford and Owen were both asleep in their car seats. I carried Ford, still dressed in his red and blue costume, inside the house. As he rested his sleepy head on my shoulder in that way that toddlers do, I began to wish he had never heard of Superman.

Does he really think he needs to save the world? And if so, does it come from the fact that his father is gone most of the time, and I am left alone?

This is a tricky, yet seldom discussed, subject for military families. When a parent is alone, it's a natural tendency to ask the children for help. And while it may be appropriate for me to expect Ford to pick-up his toys and put away his own clothes, is it really OK for him to feel like he is saving the whole world?

I struggle with these urges constantly. It feels natural to say, "Ford, you need to help Mommy while Daddy is gone," but how does that make a three-year old feel? And can Ford really distinguish between "helping" Mommy and *supporting* Mommy? When I say I need his "help," does this convey to Ford as "saving the world"?

I laid the sleepy Man of Steel on his bed for a nap. Before I left the room, I turned on a nightlight ... because my Superman is afraid of the dark, you know. He's also afraid of trampolines, swimming pools and big slides. He likes to have his pancakes cut into fourths, a Happy Meal makes his day, and he still cries if I forget to pack a special note inside his lunchbox.

Children

Ford may think he's Superman out saving the world, but he's still a little boy to me. And as long as I can keep that separate in my own mind, I suppose it's alright to let him wear his cape to school tomorrow.

Faster Than A Speeding Bullet

I was walking down our street the other day when I saw a little boy dressed in Superman pajamas toddling to the curb with his grandmother. The cape attached to his shoulders flapped in the wind like a cheap sheet, but he didn't care. With official Superman clothes hanging—and I do mean hanging—from his body, I knew the boy believed, without hesitation, that he could bend steel.

My two oldest boys, Ford, 6, and Owen, 4, spent a full year in Superman pajamas. I had to buy several sets just to keep up with the laundry. On Halloween, I begged them to pick different costumes. "Halloween is about pretending to be something you're not," I had said. "You're Superman every day, why not give Bert and Ernie a try?" It never worked. Ford was so convinced of his Superman-like traits, he styled his hair with one curl of bangs hanging in the front.

Today, Ford and Owen are what we call "closet" Superman lovers. They'd rather be caught watching "Blue's Clues" than have a neighbor see them running down the driveway in their dress-up pajamas. But that doesn't mean that they don't still covet Superman underwear. They're just a little more discreet. (Back in the day, Ford used to wear his red underwear on the outside of his pants to get a more genuine Superman effect. And I took him to the grocery store like that.)

A few years ago, when I was still washing Superman capes every single night, I thought the phase would never end. My ultimate fear was that Ford and Owen would one day wear blue tights and a red cape to high school. I began to worry that the alter-ego thing was messing with their heads. My husband and I set rules about how much time they could spend as Superman ... until I gave that idea more thought (imagine a thirty-year-old sitting in his office, legs covered in shiny blue tights and propped on the desk, telling his secretary, "Jane, hold my calls; I've got ten more minutes as Superman.")

Just when I believed that we'd have to change Owen's name to Clark and Ford's to Kal-El (Superman's Kryptonian name), which was coincidentally the same time that the boys' pants became too short and their knees grew knobby, I brought home Superman toothbrushes, and Ford and Owen told me they wanted Batman.

Excuse me?

And just like that, a piece of their childhood was gone.

I folded Ford and Owen's old Superman shirts and tucked them away in their new baby brother's drawer. The familiar yellow emblems on the front were cracked and faded with wear. There were holes in the armpits. I sat down on the floor and laughed. I could still so plainly see Ford and Owen running through the front yard, capes horizontal with the ground, on their way to save the day...or the dog, whichever. I cried holding one of the soft cotton shirts to my chest. When Dustin came into the room, he said, "My gosh, you'll be a mess when they go off to college some day."

Every one said this would happen. Old ladies at the mall used to hang over the stroller and tell me, "They grow up so fast, just you wait!" My mom said, "Before you know it they'll be all grown-up." Ford and Owen aren't there yet, but for the first time, I'm beginning to see what everyone tried to tell me: time goes by faster than ... well, faster than a speeding bullet. It seems like just yesterday that I lived with two little Supermen. Eventually, today will seem like yesterday, too.

After our third son was born this January, the doctor said to me, "Well, I guess you know what to do with this one."

And I do.

I'll start him on Superman early.

I'll take more pictures.

I'll worry less.

And I'll enjoy more.

Because I know one day, far too soon, I'll bring home a Superman toothbrush and it will be the wrong one.

What Happened To Oranges And Water?

I've recently failed at a basic (even if it is relatively new) task of motherhood: after-game snacks. And I blame time—specifically, having too much of it.

If you have a son or daughter involved in youth sports, you already know the pressure. After registering your child for a team, spending their college savings on a uniform, equipment, and the obligatory parent T-Shirt that reads "I'm [your child's name here]'s Mom," the next thing you're asked to do is sign up for snack duty. Yes, after your child has done an incredibly healthy thing, such as run around a soccer field for an hour, he or she is apparently then entitled to a snack and drink as a "reward."

When I was a kid, "snack and drink" amounted to sliced oranges and cold water dispensed out of a large cooler into those tiny paper cups that disintegrated in your hand after the sides collapsed on themselves. Today, "snack and drink" means cupcakes, full-size bottles of Gatorade, fudge-striped cookies, Doritoes, Sprite, and sometimes, ice cream. Mothers have even been known to bring cellophane bags filled with candy, much like the goody bags children receive at a birthday party.

The tone (which is to say, the expectation) for snack duty is usually set by whatever the first mother on the list brings. Unfortunately, the first mother on the list is almost always the Team Mom, or someone else more organized than me to have come up with a list in the first place. This mother is, by default, apt to bring something fantastic for the after-game snack. (Although I'd be willing to bet it won't be sliced oranges, a cooler of water, and cheap paper cups.) What this means for you, the further-down-the-list mother, is that you will be looked upon with disgust, pity, and threats of Child Protective Services if when it is your turn for snack duty, you bring raisins and bottles of water. Trust me.

"They've just played soccer for an hour, and she brings them raisins," the other mothers (the ones who brought homemade cupcakes) will think.

I'm sorry, but I'm doing good just to get my kids to the game on time (if their shoes are tied, that's a bonus). I wouldn't even know how to transport cupcakes without smashing them, and I certainly don't know how to bring ice cream and keep it frozen. But really, why do these kids need cookies, cupcakes and ice cream just because they've played a game? What happened to tousling their hair and saying, "Good job, Son. Now go take out the trash."?

At a time when our society is obsessed with the health and diets of children, when we are told that an outstanding amount of children suffer from diabetes and obesity, I'm surprised that no one is talking about this after-game snack phenomenon. Which isn't to say that I don't have a theory as to why we aren't talking about it, because I always have theories. My theory for this has to do with time. Not a lack of time, but too much of it.

Do you realize that today's mothers actually have more time than ever before? Think about all the ways in which our lives have become easier: dishwashers, fast food, microwaves, disposable diapers, washing machines. Time that my grandmother spent hanging up cloth diapers is now spent out-performing other mothers with after-game snacks. I can't help but think this isn't a good thing. The out-performing each other part, at least.

We simply have too much time today. We have time to worry about every sniffle and every statistic. We even have time to read and reread books about every developmental stage. "I didn't know about all these goofy things when I was raising kids," my 87-year-old grandmother, Doris, is known to say. "I was just doing the best I could." Doris was a young mother (like I am now) in the post-WWII era. Unlike me, Doris had very little time to worry about after-game snacks, or even sports, and certainly, she didn't have time to worry about the developmental aspects of youth sports. My uncle and

Mom were playing kickball in the front yard while she hung clothes out to dry in the back.

I'm tempted to say Doris' way is the better way. I'm also tempted to take a stand against after-game snacks at tee-ball this spring.

Yet, come to think of it, baking cupcakes for the soccer team might be annoying, but it sure beats the heck out of cleaning dirty cloth diapers and staying home all day to make meatloaf and wax the floors—especially if no other mothers have to see my dirty floors and comment about how clean theirs are.

Batman's Pants Are Painted On

Last week, I read a report from the *Washington-Post* titled, "Toy Makers Struggle to Attract Girls," which got me thinking about my own kids, Ford, 5, and Owen, 3, who are definitely not girls, and as it turns out, not the subject of Margaret Webb Pressler's article either. (Apparently there is no depletion of boy toy-buyers; while girls are moving on and advancing at the speed of technology, little boys, God love 'em, are hanging on to their Spiderman action figures and super-gusher water pistols for as long as they can, or at least, until they're twenty.)

You see, Pressler's piece uncovers the phenomenon of girls dismissing traditional toys by the time they are eight-years old, and of toy makers' attempts to win them back, keeping the cash flowing straight from Mom's wallet to their own. Apparently, according to Pressler, Barbie, who has always been the classic 8- to 9-year-old girl's toy, is now being discarded to younger sisters' closets, sisters who don't have the skilled fingers and fine motor skills to dress Barbie's thin waist and long legs. The article points out that this pushing down—much like the way kindergarten is now first grade and preschool is kindergarten—is causing one vexing dilemma: Mom's are tired of dressing Barbie for their three-year-old daughters!

Quite honestly, I had never given this grave concern much thought. My sons' Batman and Superman have their clothes painted on them. Even the superheroes' shoes are permanently affixed to their feet.

But boys' toys aren't as wonderful as they may seem, even though experts claim boys are more likely to stay in the toy market until they are twelve years old, a notion with which any one married to a man would like to disagree. While moms of girls are dressing Barbie for their preschoolers and wondering why their middle-school child is more interested in Bratz, moms of boys are telling their four-year olds, "No you can't play with that water gun. I don't care if you're pretending to be a cowboy!" Girls might be growing up, but boys are growing down.

Boys have been playing "war" and "cowboys and Indians" since the beginning of boys. Only now parents are expected to discourage such behavior. "Why don't you color a picture," we're supposed to say. "Instead of expressing your fears through aggression, Ford, why don't you share your feelings using this hand puppet?"

Yeah, I'm one of "those moms." When I sit down to play "Star Wars" with Ford and Owen, I make all the storm troopers hug before they march off to battle. And when my Princess Leia talks to Luke and Darth Vader about conflict resolution, let me tell you, it is legendary good-parenting stuff. Unfortunately, the boys usually kick me out of their play before I can get to the part where everyone agrees that weapons are bad and donates their light sabers to others in the galaxy without electricity.

Let's face it, our boys would rather chomp on a peanut butter and jelly sandwich like a saber tooth tiger eating its prey than they would hear us say, "chew with your mouth closed, Honey." Even my husband, who is a thirty-year-old child and a highly trained military pilot, does an impressive imitation of T-Rex, stomping through the house, eating imaginary pterodactyls and burping.

My point is, if we are to believe the notion in this article, little girls are maturing faster than they should, and they are abandoning baby dolls and soft toy puppies for things like glitter lipstick. But don't grieve for the loss of childhood just yet: apparently, boys are expected to take girls' place as the kinder, gentler sex. As much as I have tried to jump on this parenting band wagon (I don't want to be the only mother who lets her boys play with fire-breathing dragons, do I?), my boys are hardwired to be ... well, boys. I think this has something to do with their father, but I'm not sure.

Of course, it's responsible to teach children about kindness and sensitivity ... within the context of the child's world. Ford and Owen never even imagined people would kill one another until I brought it up in one of my hand puppet lectures about weapons. They didn't know the words "hell" or "damn" until I told them they were bad.

So I'm giving up on the hug fest and putting away the therapy puppets. I'm going to let my boys be innocent as long as they might, while staying open and available for their questions as they grow. And I'm going to be glad that Ford and Owen have the chance to remain toy-playing kids until they are twelve ... maybe longer.

Oh, and I'm also going to be glad that they've never showed any interest in glitter lipstick.

As Happy As My Saddest Child

My mom has always said, "Mothers are only as happy as their saddest child." I don't know if she coined the phrase or heard it somewhere else, but whenever I'm feeling down because one of my boys is sick, discouraged or having a hard time, I know that my mom was right. I will never be any happier than my saddest child.

For the last six weeks, everyone in my family has been sick. During a four-week stretch, my boys alternated being home from school due to illnesses. I was beginning to feel claustrophobic and Dustin couldn't understand why. He of course still went to work every day and even made a trip—for "flight-training purposes"—to Key West.

It all started back in October when Owen had a blocked intestine (hope you weren't eating) which resolved just in time for the already scheduled surgery to remove his tonsils and adenoids in November. The next two weeks were a blur as Owen slowly recovered and Dustin, home for a few hours each night, made comments like, "Wow, it's draining when they're sick, isn't it?" (This kind of reminded me of how he once said that the "most tired" he's ever been was when I was in labor.)

Owen rallied in time for Thanksgiving, and our lives were getting back to normal, if only for 24 hours. Then Ford got pneumonia— twice.

It was around this time that Dustin made his trip to Key West for training. When he called from a noisy street corner to tell me about the great restaurants and bars, I couldn't wait to tell him about all the "excitement" here at home: I had folded five loads of laundry, Ford had a fever, and Owen went to the bathroom on the floor three times.

Yes, I was angry that Dustin wasn't home to help. I even yelled at him over the phone, reminding him of all the times he's been gone—on deployment or on "training missions" to the most sought-after vacation destinations—just when we need him the most.

All Dustin said was, "I promise, I wish I was there."

He would rather be home with sick kids than hooping it up in Key West? I didn't believe him.

Yet, as my anger wore off, I realized that as bad as it had been the past six weeks, there's no place else I would have rather been than at home with Ford and Owen. I couldn't imagine being in Key West or Paris or even Hawaii when one of my children is sick and needs me.

Our service member spouses miss a lot while they are gone, and sometimes it seems unfair that they miss more than their share of nights spent awake with a sick child and harried trips to the emergency room. In our desperation, we might actually believe our spouses rejoice in what seems like deliberately shirked responsibilities. But the truth is, we have become so focused on their absences at Christmas, birthdays and other happy occasions, we forget that perhaps the hardest time to be away from home is when your family needs you. If we think missing Thanksgiving is bad, imagine being halfway across the world when your son is in the hospital.

My guess is that many service members would trade all the missed anniversaries and birthdays just to be home every time their child was sick or their spouse was crying on the living room floor.

On the phone, I acted as if Dustin was purposefully M.I.A. when we needed him. What he tried to tell me, but I couldn't hear at the time, was that as beautiful and fun as Key West may be, it's nothing compared to being home with your family to help them through the bad times. He wasn't celebrating the fact that he had dodged the midnight-shift with a feverish Ford. Instead, he was trying to get home as soon as possible.

Because even when you're on vacation—oops, excuse me; when you're on a training mission—in a sunny place like South Florida, you're still only as happy as your saddest child.

Fear Of Flying
Might Not Be Hereditary

The sky rumbled as I packed Ford's suitcase. It wasn't outright thunder. No, it was much more ominous than that. It was a grumble, like a lone bowling ball rolling through the clouds. And it hadn't even rained yet. Still, as I folded each little shirt and placed it in the blue suitcase, I couldn't help but think, "I'm glad I'm not getting on an airplane tomorrow."

And then, a small voice in the back of my head said, "Yes, but your child is."

I've been a fearful flyer my entire life. In fact, I've only flown twice: once when I was a baby and too young to know better, and once nine years ago when I was dating my soon-to-be husband and would blindly follow him anywhere (especially to Hawaii for a week). But I haven't flown since 1997, and after September 11, 2001, I sometimes think I never will again.

Apparently I'm in good company because according to Airfraid.com, nearly 25 million Americans are also afraid to fly. However, it's surprising that I'm one of them because both my husband and my father are Navy pilots. I've grown up around airplanes and aircraft carriers. I've quizzed my husband on his "emergency procedures" during flight school. And on hundreds of mornings, I've waved goodbye as he set off to work ... in a helicopter. But I've seldom worried about him being up in the air. Not on a daily basis, at least, and not to the point where my stomach is in knots and my face is full of tears.

So when a family wedding was planned in Seattle, Wash., this summer, it was easy for me to say, "You just go, Dustin, and I'll stay home." It feels natural to send my husband off in an airplane, and I knew I wouldn't worry about him. My logical brain understands that statistically flying is safe. But my emotional, irrational brain believes that I can't handle eight hours of intense fear. I'm less afraid of flying than I am of being afraid.

All was good and exceedingly normal, until Ford decided to go on the trip with his dad. Ford was nervous, but curious. For several weeks leading up to the trip, he went back and forth between, "No, I don't think I'll go," and "Mom, do you think I'll be OK if I go?" It took all I had in me to smile and tell my son with the big brown eyes, "Yes, you will be fine. I promise."

It's one thing not to shed a tear when you send a grown husband off in an airplane to a city across the country (especially when that husband makes his living flying and has been 5-6 time zones away from you while he was on deployment). But it's quite another thing entirely to send your 5-year-old son up into the air with his mother's promise that everything will be OK. My husband knows the risks and makes his own decisions. My son trusts me to keep him safe, and I was about to put him in an airplane, the thing I fear most.

"If something happens to him," I said to Dustin, "I would never forgive myself for telling him that he'd be fine."

I folded Ford's Superman pajamas and put them in the suitcase on the bed. He's basically outgrown the blue and red set, but I knew he'd want it to feel brave. As I smoothed out the folds in his dress pants, Ford said, "Mom, I don't think I'll go away to college because I always want to live with you."

"That's very sweet," I said, "but when you're older, you'll change your mind."

"No," he said. "I always want to live with you."

I put Rocket, Ford's favorite stuffed animal who smells like drool and has one grimy ear where Ford rubs him, into the suitcase and zipped it shut. The next morning, before we got to the airport, Dustin told me, "Try not to cry because it will make it harder for Ford."

"OK," I said biting my already trembling lip.

But when I hugged Ford goodbye, the tears came.

"It's OK," Ford said. "I'll be back in a few days."

As I watched him walk down the airport terminal and disappear into a crowd of people, I wondered to myself, *how many more times will I watch him leave?* First this trip, then the school bus, then his driver's license, then prom, and then college. And always, I am sure, I will stand there crying ... even though Dustin has told me not to.

Yes, Ford is outgrowing his Superman pajamas, but he is becoming a different kind of hero to me. He is becoming a brave young boy who tries new things, things I may never do. And he is on his way to becoming the kind of man who smiles and tells his tearful Mom, "I'll be OK," then turns around to begin the life she has always wanted him to have.

The Last Time I Held You

We sat down in the pew together, you in your new button-down shirt and clip-on tie, looking so much like your dad, who was at the back of the church, standing as an usher. You set your cheek against my arm and leaned into me like a puppy finding his favorite spot on a pillow. I smoothed the tuft of hair sticking up above your ear and checked, for the billionth time, to see if the spot of eczema on top of your scalp has healed.

I know your head—your hair, your hands—like I know my own skin. The doughy feeling of your forehead and the small flat beds of your nails are as familiar to me as my own cowlick or the gap between my two bottom teeth. I can distinguish the sound of your breathing from that of your brother, Owen.

I can tell, by scent alone, when you are sick.

The choir hadn't finished singing the first song before you wriggled away from my side and lay face down on the red cushioned pew. "Ford, sit up," I whispered through clenched teeth.

"But I'm bored," you said.

I handed you a bulletin and flipped it around so that you could draw on the blank side of the paper. Then I searched through my purse for a pen. Maybe two. Ten minutes later, the pew beside me looked like it had thrown up. Paper—all with sketches of Batman in various states of rescue on them—were strewn across the seat, and pens littered the floor like spilled toothpicks. Your new tie was smashed between the cushions, and you had pulled the hem of your shirt out of your pants.

The minister called for the final hymn and the congregation stood to sing. "Hold me," you said, and I obliged.

Perched on my hip, you towered above my head. When you were

a baby, you fit on my side and curled across my chest to rest your head on my collar. Now you sit upon my arm like an awkward, hooved animal who's cumbersome to carry. I remember when your bottom, padded with a diaper, was a round pillow on my hip. How your shoulders and back and legs were one pudgy mass. Like a bag of sugar, you'd mold yourself into my embrace. But now your legs are like fledgling twigs, and your body is as solid and heavy as a brick. You tried to put your arms around me and leaned your head down to meet my shoulder, but the position was awkward, like an adult stuffing themselves into a child's chair.

And it was then that I realized, with a very heavy heart, that soon I will carry you for the last time. I will still be able to hug you, to ruffle your hair and pat your leg, but I will not be able to lift you onto my hip and hold you like a baby.

The service ended and Daddy came to get you. "Want to help me clean up the pews," he said, and the two of you set off across the church, with you galloping at his side.

I stood alone beside my seat, somehow more naked and cold, and thought about the months we spent together, just you and I, while Daddy was deployed. For nearly two years I carted you everywhere I went. There wasn't more than eight hours that we spent apart. Sometimes, even when I was so tired I felt my bones ache, I couldn't get up to put you in your crib, and we fell asleep together on the living room couch—you nestled into the crook of my arm, your wispy baby hair brushing against my cheek.

Often, I didn't know where you ended and I began.

On my way to get Owen at the church nursery, I found you with Dad in the hallway. "Can I hold you for a second?" I said, and you lifted up your arms. I hugged you close and kissed your head. But you couldn't have known, because I didn't say, that in my mind I was memorizing the feel of your cheeks, still full of baby fat, and the sight of your skin, untouched by the sun and as smooth as the bottom of a baby's foot.

You may be lanky and long and sprouting like a tree, but you are still so much a child.

My child.

I set you on the floor again and you ran to meet your brother.

I can not begin to count the times that I have carried you, lifted you, hugged you. I've trekked hundreds of miles with you on my hip. But today, I put your feet on the floor and watched you run, satisfied to the depths of my being that I will hold you forever in a way that only a mother can understand.

Children:

WHEN WAS THE LAST TIME YOU BUMPED HEADS?

Flamingoes Don't Stand On Two Legs

Our world is a small one. You knew that. But did you know that the world becomes significantly smaller (which is to say, as small as an elevator feels when your infant son has just messed his pants) when your husband's boss lives in the house behind yours?

Dustin's boss, or "CO" in Navy speak, is a wonderful man with a great sense of humor (remember that because it becomes important later), but that doesn't mean Dustin isn't slightly unnerved knowing that the CO can look across his yard and see Dustin putting the wrong fertilizer on our grass. And we have children, too, which throws all kinds of variables into the mix. Dustin can tell me to quit leaving on the flood lights—the ones that shine right into the CO's house—all night (actually, I think his exact words were, "If you leave those lights on again, I'll rip the entire light fixture out of the wall"), but when it comes to our three boys, well, Dustin can talk all he wants ("Stop hitting baseballs into the CO's yard!" and "If you're going to moon each other, could you do it in the front yard, please?"), and it doesn't mean they will listen.

Which brings us to two weeks ago.

Dustin was leaving for work early one morning, when the dew was still on the grass and clinging to ... the six pink flamingoes in our front yard?

"Sarah," he yelled back into the house. "Do you know anything about the pink flamingoes in our yard? The ones with bows around their necks." (As if there is any other kind.)

Apparently we had been "flamingoed." A large poster-board sign next to the birds told us that a high-school group raising money for their graduation party was responsible. In order to get the flamingoes out of our yard and into someone else's, we had to pay $10.00. If we didn't want the flamingoes to ever flock our yard again, we could pay an extra $5.00. And who sent us these six pink treasures? The CO and his wife, of course. And they have a teenaged daughter, so Dustin worried (without reason; the CO had been an unwitting "victim," just like us) that it might be her school or friends raising the money.

"Whatever you do, don't let anything happen to those flamingoes today," Dustin said as he left for work.

The children were of course delighted to see the tacky pink birds in our yard. I can only guess now, in hindsight, that they spent a good majority of the school day imagining what they would do to the flamingoes when they got home.

The bird's instructions said that their owner (not related to the CO in any way) would be back at 8:00 p.m. to pick up the flock, our check, and directions to the next sucker—I mean donator—of our choosing. At 4:00, however, just one hour after my older boys, Ford, 7, and Owen, 5, had gotten home from school, there was a knock on the door. A flustered woman stood on the front porch, one lone pink bird clutched to her chest.

"I've come to pick up the birds," she said flatly.

"Oh, let me write a check then," I said. "I'm sorry that I'm not ready yet. I thought you guys weren't coming until later."

"Usually, yes. But we got a call from an anonymous source saying that your children were beating the flamingoes in the front yard." She made a motion like swinging a baseball bat with her free arm.

I was confused because I knew that Owen was asleep on the couch, and I thought Ford was upstairs. But just then, Ford and our neighbor's son peeked around the side of the house, guilt all over their faces.

"Oh, those children," I said, pointing to Ford and his friend. "I have no idea who those children are."

The lady wasn't buying it.

I spent the next hour helping her and the boys unearth buried flamingo parts in our front yard. Then I wrote a big check to help cover the cost of the damaged birds.

When Dustin got home that night, together we grilled Ford about his behavior. Ford sobbed into his hands. "But flamingoes are only supposed to stand on one leg," he said. "And those birds were standing on two, so we pulled off the extra ones and buried them."

He had a point. Flamingoes do only stand on one leg.

Still, I knew by the look on Dustin's face that if I value his sanity at all (and often I do), I would definitely turn off the flood lights before going to bed.

Big Heads, Small Shirts

Both of my sons must have extraordinarily large heads. I say this because there isn't a single shirt that I can get on them without stretching out the neck first. Every morning it's the same thing: first I argue with the boys about which shirts they can wear ("No, you can't wear your Batman top again today," and, "You've chewed the sleeve off that sweater so we'll have to throw it away.") then, I take the shirt that meets my approval, place it in my two hands, and pull like all get out to make the neck hole big enough for their head.

And still I have to tug and pull on the hem, until the boys' ears are pinned against their necks and their cheeks are flattened beneath the shirt's collar. Sometimes the boys can't take it any more and they run away before the neck hole has safely cleared the bridge of their nose (in my experience, the hardest part to cross). They dance around the bedroom, often hopping from foot to foot and looking like a headless monster, as they yell, "It's too tight! It's too tight!"

Don't bother suggesting that I buy different size shirts for Ford and Owen. It doesn't matter how big the rest of the shirt may be, the neck will always be too small. I'm beginning to think these tiny collars are a ploy of the clothing industry to make kids grow out of their shirts even faster than they already do. Because really, when was the last time you as an adult had trouble pulling a shirt over your head? This seems to be a problem unique to children under the age of ten.

And while we're speaking of heads, it seems that toddlers also have a habit of "bumping heads" on a regular, sometimes daily, basis. Ford and Owen can be playing 10-feet away from each other, and still they will manage to bump their heads. Even if children are in a room alone, they will go out and seek another head to bump. A few weeks

Children

ago, I was mopping the laundry room floor when all of the sudden, I looked up and bumped heads with Ford. I didn't even know he was in the same room. In fact, we weren't in the same room until that moment. Somehow, Ford sensed that I was about to lift my head, and so he came over to bump it with his own.

I ask you, when was the last time that you, as an adult, bumped heads with another person who wasn't three-feet tall?

There are just some things that are unique to children, and somewhere along the line, we adults grow out of them (and our shirts).

Take puddles, for instance. My sons' feet are like magnets for water. They will go out of their way to step in a giant puddle of mud. And also gum. If there is gum on the street, they will step in it. They jump off the porch and don't break their ankle. They slide on the hardwood floors and don't get hurt. They get the hiccups every time they eat, and—this is what gets me the most, by the way—their hair always looks cute. Even with bed-head.

The other day, I watched as Ford and Owen played on the driveway.

When was the last time I thought of our driveway as a three-ring circus? I wondered.

I watched as Ford and Owen collected sticks.

When was the last time sticks were something else besides "yard debris"?

I watched as they ran through the sprinkler and laughed at being wet.

When was the last time my clothes got soaked and I didn't worry about washing them?

Later that same day, Ford and Owen asked for sidewalk chalk to draw on the driveway. With the sun on our backs and ants crawling across our bare feet, I sat on the concrete next to my boys and traced the outline of my hand with a big piece of pink chalk.

And I couldn't remember the last time I had done that.

The Best Of Both Worlds

It's hard to believe that one year ago I announced to you the birth of our third son, Lindell, born on January 9, 2007. Not to sound like my mom, but well, where did the time go? And why didn't my baby weight go with it?

Perhaps it's selfish, but a baby's first birthday is often more about the mother than it is about the child. A baby doesn't understand parties. To them, their birthday is just another day. For the mother, however, it marks a bittersweet milestone. They have made it through the first year—a feat that requires an unusual compilation of skills, including being able to cook spaghetti with one hand, staying awake for 20 hours at a time, and removing soiled onsies without getting any of the "soil" on the baby's head—but they are also about to say goodbye to the most brief and precious twelve months of their child's life.

This concept of having mixed emotions about the end of a baby's first year couldn't have come into more focus than during the days leading up to Lindell's birthday. First, he had an ear infection. The only time Lindell wasn't crying was when he was eating or sleeping, and he did neither very often. The day before his birthday, Lindell had a doctor's appointment. On the way to the hospital, he had— how can I say this delicately?—a stomach ache all over his car seat. One new diaper and change of clothes later, he did it again in the waiting room, this time, all over my pants and shirt, too. I didn't have any more clothes for Lindell, so he went into the exam room naked. I, unfortunately, did not have that option. (And I say "unfortunately" because at this point, I would have gladly worn a diaper or a onesie, anything except my clothes, which were so dirty and smelly, people were running away from me.) When we left the hospital, I knew that someday—maybe when Lindell is 16 and driving—this would be funny. But not then.

At some point during all of this, Dustin told me that he had to work on the night of Lindell's birthday. Lindell is our third child, so unlike with the other two, I had no fantasies of something close to a small wedding planned for Lindell's birthday. I simply wanted to mark the occasion with a cake and whatever family we could round-up (a difficult task for military families who are spread out across the country and rarely live near Grandma and Grandpa). Dustin missed so much of Ford and Owen's first years while he was on deployment, it has been an unexpected and almost indulgent experience to have him here for all of Lindell's. And now Dustin was going to miss the grande finale? When I said I wanted Lindell's party to be "low key," I didn't mean that anyone related to the birthday boy who wasn't currently deployed didn't need to do everything in his power to be there. The news did not go over well.

Yet, then I realized that when Dustin was gone during our other boys' first years, it was on the normal days that I felt his absence most. Forget birthdays, I wanted Dustin there for the long haul. I wanted him there for the eating-Cheerioes-going-for-a-walk-and-having-a-bubble-bath kind of days. This time we had the reverse. Dustin was here for all the other days, so how could I be upset if he missed the birthday party?

I settled into the idea of celebrating Lindell's birthday without Dustin. I made a cake shaped like a carousel, and the boys and I planned to take it up to the church to celebrate with friends. I reminded myself to be thankful for all the days Dustin has been home this year and not to be so greedy as to want him there for the party, too.

Then, at the last minute, Dustin was able to come home early and meet us at the church. He was there to sing Happy Birthday and to feed Lindell cake. And in that moment, I felt like the luckiest military wife around, because for once, I had the best of both worlds.

Fighting The British In Our Front Yard

There is a book titled "The Dangerous Book for Boys" (Harper Collins), by brothers Conn and Hal Iggulden, that teaches boys how to, basically, have a childhood. This having a childhood stuff used to come naturally to boys. (Maybe they are evolving?) In the book, there are lessons on fishing, building forts and go-karts, and identifying spiders and insects. The great success of "The Dangerous Book for Boys" suggests that many young boys don't already know how to turn sticks into pretend guns or chase little girls with lizards and grasshoppers.

I have three boys. Not one of them needs this book.

Just the other day, I was clipping dead blooms off the rose bush when Ford came around the corner with a wooden musket hanging from his shoulder by a leather strap. He was wearing the triangle-shaped felt hat (the one he calls the "George Washington hat") that we bought in Williamsburg, Va., and cost us more than our lunch. But he was wearing the hat backwards, so it looked more like a felt sailor's cover than it did something from the Revolutionary War.

"You're gonna have to move, Mom," Ford said. "The British are coming, and we've got a war to fight."

Just then, our neighbor's boy peeked around the bushes. He looked suspiciously British.

"Right here in the front yard?" I asked. "Can't you have a war in the backyard?"

Apparently, they could not. You see, the Potomac River, that thin strip of white concrete that connects our driveway to our front door, is indisputably in the front yard, not the back, and it can't be moved. Also, our front yard, once the burial place for the body parts of several plastic flamingoes left in our grass for a fundraiser and promptly destroyed by my son (because "flamingoes aren't supposed to stand on two legs anyway"), is the boys' preferred place to play, mostly because—I'm sure of it—their dad and I paid the equivalent of several felt hats from Williamsburg to have a large backyard with a fence. Although, the boys' fondness for the front yard might also be because they like to show all of our neighbors how they play tee-ball barefooted, hang from the mailbox, pull each other through the grass with a jumprope (not recommended), and sometimes, urinate in the dirt.

Before I moved to the backyard to make way for the Revolutionary War, I wanted to finish pruning the roses and take limbs off the River Birch, because of course, I want our front yard to look nice when the boys are beating each other on the ground.

As quick as I laid cut limbs on the grass, the boys were hauling them off to their "fort" and pretending they were swords. But my middle son, Owen, 5, who thinks jokes involving his bodily functions are the ultimate in humor, doesn't understand the Revolutionary War the same way that Ford, 7, (he once read the phone book just for fun) does.

"I'm going to get a gun from the garage," Owen told Ford.

I looked around for passersby, ready to assure them that my boys weren't talking about real guns. Just another one of those tricky aspects of parenting in today's world. Except, explaining toy guns would be much easier, I thought, than those times I had to explain why Owen yells "Let's get Trojan ready" in the front yard. (Answer: his tee-ball team is named "Trojans".)

"They're not guns," Ford yelled at Owen. "They're muskets!"

Owen came back with a battery-operated laser gun that has a siren.

Ford threw his felt hat at the ground and stomped his foot. "Oweeeeen!" he yelled. "They didn't have laser guns back then! And their guns didn't have sirens! We're talking about, like, 100 years ago!"

I looked up from my pruning. "Actually, it was more than 200 years ago, Ford," I said.

Owen went back to the garage and came out with a football

helmet on his head.

"What are you doing now?" Ford asked.

"I'll be the helicopter pilot," Owen said. "I'll shoot down the bad guys."

"They didn't have helicopters either!" Ford was screaming now. "Come on, grab a musket, and let's fight the South."

"The British," I corrected. "The North fought the South in the Civil War."

"Whatever."

Owen pointed his laser gun at me and asked if I was British.

I finished my yard work while the boys slid on their bellies through the "swamps" of the battlefield and chased down run-away Big Wheels ... I mean, horses. They continued to fight, alternately, the South and the British, and eventually, Ford gave up and let Owen use his laser gun with the siren.

No, my boys don't need a book to learn about being dangerous. But that day, when the Revolutionary War, Civil War and Gulf War were all seemingly fought simultaneously on our freshly mowed lawn, I realized that perhaps what my boys do need is a history book.

What A Difference A Year Has Made

By now you already know quite a bit about my oldest son, Ford, who will turn seven years old on Thanksgiving Day. You might not, however, know as much about my second son, Owen, who will celebrate his fifth birthday two days later. That's because Owen has the unfortunate honor bestowed upon second children everywhere: his scrapbook is half as thick, his clothes are half as new, and his time in the spotlight is half as much. This isn't intentional, of course, and if Owen should ever think much of his plight, he need only talk to our third son, Lindell, who doesn't even have a scrapbook yet.

I've been thinking a lot about Owen lately because never before has there been one of my children's birthdays that has surprised me more. For seven years, Ford has progressively grown and matured with no exceptional spurts or stalls. At his fifth birthday, he wasn't that much different from the year before. Like a shrub that seems to not change at all, until years later when you see an old picture of the front yard and say, "Wow, look at how small the plants were," Ford has grown, emotionally and physically, in a steady, almost imperceptible, way. Owen has been more like a sunflower. One day you see a sprout pushing its way through the earth, and the next day there is tall skinny stalk swaying in the breeze.

A year ago today, when Owen was 4 years old, he was still wearing diapers and I was trying to hide that fact from his preschool, where the rules state that any child outside of the two-year-old class must be potty-trained. Owen was also wearing a size 2T shirt and size 12-months pants. His weight teetered between 25-28 pounds. (For comparison, my 10-month-old baby currently weighs 20 pounds). Owen rarely talked, he cried when I left him at school, and he preferred sitting in my lap to doing just about anything else. He had permanent dark circles under his eyes.

But a mother usually doesn't see these things. He was simply Owen—the boy who, when he was a baby, I liked to call a little kitten because he was so small—and he had always been that way. He had always needed extra help, smaller clothes, and a large amount of exception ("Sure he should be potty-trained by now, but he's Owen, and well ... "). I didn't even think much of it when people constantly asked if Owen was sick. It wasn't until a doctor at the Navy hospital suggested that Owen have his tonsils and adenoids removed that I began to realize maybe there really was something wrong.

Two weeks before Owen's tonsilectomy and adenoidectomy, he was in the emergency room with a blocked intestine. That cleared up, quite literally, just in time (two days before) the oral surgery. Then, as soon as Owen had recovered from the surgery, he got pneumonia. His weight was dipping closer to 20 pounds at this point, and even the 2T clothes weren't fitting. My mom likes to say that a mother is only as happy as her saddest child, and this was never more apparent than last winter. I remember those weeks between Halloween and New Year's as being nothing but dark.

But like the sunflower poking through the dirt, Spring came and Owen started to change. The dark circles were gone. He was gaining weight. And seemingly overnight, Owen basically potty-trained himself.

Before the surgery, Owen's doctor had told us, "He'll be like a different kid after this." I was skeptical. In December, I looked at Owen and thought, "Looks the same (which is to say, just as small, just as sick) to me." Last night at dinner, one full year later, I looked across the table and saw a little boy; not "Owen the baby," and not Owen-who-is-as-small-as-a-kitten, but Owen ... my little boy. A little boy who suddenly has cheekbones where baby fat used to be, knobby knees that touch in the middle, and a nose that is finally taking shape and looking so much like my husband's.

This week, Owen will have the biggest speaking part in the preschool Thanksgiving play. It is a part for which he volunteered. Yes, the boy who one year ago was still wearing diapers and hardly spoke a word has now volunteered to stand in front of an audience and say, "We want to welcome all of you to our Thanksgiving show."

The audience will clap and say, "How cute," but they will never know what those eleven words mean to me. Owen will welcome the group, but as his mother, what I will likely hear is, "Welcome, Mom, to the boy I've become and the man I will someday be."

Owen Drew A Masterpiece … On His Etch-A-Sketch

I can only assume that being the "middle child" feels a lot like getting cut in line every single day, or like being the last one at the table to receive their meal. I was the baby of the family, and also the only girl, so by most accounts, I had it good. My own middle child, Owen, 4, is therefore giving me newfound sympathy for "sandwiched" kids.

As the second-born, Owen gets the usual unintended slights. His scrapbook is only half as thick as his older brother Ford's. (Although, our new baby, Lindell, doesn't even have a scrapbook yet, so it's all relative). Owen rarely gets his own clothes, just a drawer full of hand-me-downs. And as soon as Owen can rightly brag about accomplishing some feat (learning his "left" and "right," coloring in the lines, putting on his own pants), Ford learns something seemingly "better" (reading the phone book and naming the 16th president). Owen is perpetually a day late and a dollar short. Never mind that Ford still can't tie his own shoes. When you're the middle kid, apparently you only see all the ways that your sibling is better than you.

It doesn't help that Ford literally never stops talking. In preschool, they gave him the Indian name Chief-Talks-A-lot. Owen was a late walker and talker, something that my husband, Dustin, and I worried about. But the doctors said that Owen had just one problem and his name begins with "F." Owen didn't need to walk or talk; Ford did it for him. While Ford gives us a daily, running dialogue about everything from his concern that Giganotosaurus might actually be larger than Tyrannosaurus Rex to his troublesome bowel movements, Owen has to be coaxed into telling us what he wants for dinner. When I talked to Ford about the importance of giving Owen a chance to speak, Ford said, "I give Owen a chance to talk when I'm asleep or eating."

It also doesn't help that Ford is a smarty-pants who was reading before Kindergarten and instinctively understood at the age of four that trees in the front of a picture should be larger than trees in the back. It's one thing to have an older brother to keep up with, quite another to have a brother who reads books like "U.S. Presidents" for fun.

I sympathize with Owen. Growing up, my older brother, Will, now a well-known artist on the east coast, constantly outdid me. At Easter, when we were dying our eggs, I thought I was ingenious to dip half the egg in yellow and half the egg in blue, so that a band in the middle became green. But then, I'd look across the kitchen table and see that Will was painting a moon and blue swirls on his egg and naming it "Starry Night," or something like that.

I naturally want to make things even between my boys, so I'm always on the lookout for ways to bolster Owen's self-esteem. Last month, I had that opportunity when he came to me and said, "Mom, look at this neat race car I drew."

Oh goody, I thought. Now I can lavish his artwork with attention and hang it on the refrigerator, just like we have done with Ford's drawings. But when I looked up from my magazine, I saw that Owen had drawn the race car on an Etch-a-Sketch. Wouldn't you know that he'd draw his first masterpiece on something that is inherently meant to be erased?

Later, I was going through old photographs and noticed that Owen's third birthday party was almost entirely overshadowed by Ford and his friends. There was only one picture of Owen alone, and no pictures of him standing next to his cake. Just a picture of Ford standing next to Owen's cake.

Several weeks ago, Owen came to me and said, "Mommy, do you think I'm a dummy? I know I'm not because you say I'm not, but sometimes I can't help thinking I am." He went on to tell me that he has nothing of his own, and then he fell asleep crying.

When I say my heart felt stomped on and broken into a million pieces, I know the parents out there understand.

I'm Just Saying...

I worried about my conversation with Owen. I tortured myself with it for days. Until sometime later, when I witnessed Ford helping Owen button his shirt. I realized then that there are worse things than being a middle child. Indeed, Ford might say being the oldest is rough. And someday, Lindell will feel cheated, too.

Yet a long time from now, when my boys are old, I hope they will realize that having a brother—any kind of brother—was better than not having one at all.

Danger Lurks At The Commissary

If you've recently had your first baby, you are about to experience a military phenomenon so shrouded in mystery and secrecy that it causes even seasoned admiral's wives to shudder when they think of it. The mere mention of this military oddity can ruin a party. Bring it up in a room full of military wives, and the ones with children will likely drop their plates and dive on their bellies in your direction, screaming "NOOO" in slow motion, as they try to hush you up.

We don't want the child-free military wives to get wind of this any more than we want them to hear what happens on the third day postpartum (namely: pregnancy hormones drop like a piano falling out of a second-story window, and you cry, scream and yell at anything or anyone, including, but not limited to, your husband, the nurse who calls you "honey," and the next person who says your baby looks just like Winston Churchhill).

It's not that we don't want other mothers to experience this secret that I'm about to reveal. We're not trying to keep it for ourselves. Oh no, quite the contrary. We don't tell unsuspecting new moms about this event because misery *does* love company, and we want the uninitiated to go through the exact same terror that we did, without fair warning. Consider it SERE (Survival, Evasion, Resistance, and Escape) school for new mothers.

By now, maybe you're afraid. And you should be. If you don't have children but think you might want them one day, I suggest you flip the page now because once you hear the truth about this, you can not get your innocence back.

Yes, it's that bad.

What we're talking about here is going to the commissary ... with children.

No one knows exactly why the commissary makes children crazy, but we are learning every day that there is something, an intangible *something*, about on-base grocery stores that makes children behave as if they have been raised by cavemen. Their behavior goes far beyond the usual put-sugary-sweets-in-the-basket-while-Mommy-isn't-looking and straight to scream-as-if-my-arm-is-being-cut-off-with-toenail-clippers.

Stand at the front of your local commissary and you can actually see this phenomenon unfold. Mothers enter the store and put their darling children with cute pigtails and denim overalls in the seat of the basket. Sometimes the mothers have special blankets that they drape over the basket's seat and handle bar so that their children won't get dirty (Ha. Ha. Ha.). If the mother's children are older, they might ride in the front of a shopping cart made to look like a race car or space ship. The mother will actually buckle these children "behind the wheel," and no matter how many times she's been shopping before, she will believe that her children will stay that way.

Off they go, down the first aisle. The mother is in control. She is calm, cool and collected. She might even have a shopping list in her hand. A few minutes later you will see the mother coming down the second aisle. She is still calm, but you might notice that one of the children has come unbuckled. Or maybe the baby has managed to get her mouth on the one spot of exposed dirty metal and is sucking on it like a pacifier.

Several aisles later, you will see the crew again. The mother is becoming disheveled. Her shopping list is tattered. Boxes of frozen pizza might slide off the mound of food piled high in her basket. When she turns to go down another aisle and out of your view, you will find that you can still hear her yelling, "This is your last warning!" and the kids shouting, "He's touching my leg! Make him stop touching my leg."

By the time you see the mother coming to the check-out line, she will look like a different woman. She will probably be covered in perspiration. Look closely and you will notice something amazing: she no longer cares that her son is sitting on the hood of the race car. If she could get that fancy, protective drape out from under the baby, she'd wrap it around her head until she could no longer hear the children.

Some people speculate that it is the overhead lights and big, warehouse atmosphere of commissaries that makes children crazy. This theory doesn't make sense, however, given that civilian grocery stores, many of which are bigger and more warehouse-like than commissaries, also have fluorescent lights.

Others have said that children are simply feeding off their mother's stress, and that unlike other shopping trips where one might just pick up a few items, the shopping list for a trip to the commissary is usually several pages long.

I used to believe the aggravation could be blamed on the automated speaker at the check-out lines that says, "Next please, next please," over and over again, heralding the next lucky shopper through the last hurdle of commissary: the bill.

But now I think the phenomenon likely has a specific purpose. After one-two hours of pulling children off the top of the race car, listening to a baby cry, and maneuvering around tight corners with a basket that has items teetering several inches above the sides, no mother, no matter how determined and purposeful she began, cares how much it will cost to get out of the commissary and back into her car. With a defeated look on their faces, they will sign a big check and hand it to the cashier, who is smiling because she is also glad the woman and her children are leaving.

And now, here is the weirdest part. Even with all of this, the woman will come back, maybe as soon as two weeks later, and do the whole thing again. Which leads me to believe that there might be an element of amnesia to this. [Begin music from "The Twilight Zone"] Although, I'm not sure. I can't remember the last time I was in the commissary, but I'm going there this week … .

Sports and School:

AND YOU THOUGHT YOU WERE DONE.

Lessons From The Dugout

You stood at the tee, staring out to the field, which seemed to reduce you to a small speck against a canvas of green grass and red, dusty baseball dirt. Part boy and part baby, your knobby knees touched in the middle, but your rounded tummy poked through the t-shirt hanging so low it covered your shorts. You raised the bat to your shoulder. The large, red batter's helmet wobbled on your head. From the splintered stands, behind home plate, I clutched my hands together.

The coaches initially suggested that we put you back in a younger league with the 4- to 5-year-olds. "He's small for his age," they had said. "He might get hurt." But I knew what they meant: Your son can't catch a ball. He doesn't run fast. And sometimes he misses when he swings.

Dad spent hours in the front yard working with you. Then he convinced the coaches to let you play with the other 6-year-olds. "Sending him back," Dad said, "will break his spirit."

Thinking back on it now, sitting behind you and separated by a metal fence at your very first game, I wondered if Dad and I had made a mistake. The other kids will laugh at him, I thought. He'll get the first out.

Someone behind me said, "That boy is so small."

A lump rose in my throat.

You took a practice swing. The other players and the spectators quieted to a few scattered whispers. All eyes were on you.

My child.

You drew the bat to your shoulder again, ready for the real thing. Please just let him get on First, I thought. It will mean the world to him.

I'm Just Saying...

You swung the bat. The motion was awkward and the bat was too high. You missed the ball. I lowered my head to hide the sudden rush of tears in my eyes. Someone from the other team laughed.

The coach patted you on the back and whispered in your ear. Then he stood back, and you pulled up the bat again. With a timid shift of your hips, you put all of your 40 pounds behind the next swing. The ball flew from the tee and landed right at the pitcher's feet. "He'll never make it to First," someone said.

Now, I'm not a screamer. I'm hardly competitive, and I don't care for sports. But right then, as your feet left home plate, I stood in my seat and yelled as loud as I could, "Run, Ford! Don't look back, just run!"

The ball beat you to the base. You were out, and the inning was over. You ran with the other kids to the dugout. I rushed to meet you, but you disappeared behind the cinderblock wall. Will the kids tease him? I wondered. Will he cry?

Dad told me to let it go. It's all part of the game, part of being a boy, he said. After many roasts at military parties, Dad knows that being part of a team means learning to roll with the punches, and that sometimes, oddly, males bond over ridicule and gentle teasing.

Do not go in the dugout, he told me.

For 10 painful minutes, you were invisible to me. I would never know what happened in the dugout. It wasn't my place. You had to learn this lesson on your own.

Sometimes, I guess, being a mother means allowing you to have experiences that will break my heart while they build your character.

You were at bat again for the last inning. We were separated by more than a metal fence now. In the dugout you had grown in ways I will never understand. You planted your feet firmly in the dirt and pulled up the bat. The coach gave you an encouraging smile. You swung, but I couldn't bear to watch. Then I heard someone yell, "Run, Ford," so I opened my eyes and saw you running to First. You made it. The crowd laughed as you did a victory dance. Two batters later, you were safe again on Third. You looked to see if I was watching. Someday, I thought, you'll look for another girl in the stands. But for now it is me. The next batter hit the ball and you ran home. Then you circled back to the dugout, leaving me there behind the fence, at home plate, where I will always be cheering for you.

He'll Play The Infield

Last year, my son Ford, then 6, was, let's face it, the worst athlete on his tee-ball team. He was also the smallest, youngest and least experienced. Not surprisingly, the coaches often stuck him in the outfield. Sometimes they left him in the dugout for whole innings.

Ford, God love him, never lost heart. At times I was sure he'd want to quit. But then, to my surprise, he was ready for every practice and standing in the outfield for every game, that characteristic half-moon smile—the one he's had to grow into since it covered half his face as a baby—shining out from the shadows of his baseball cap. He always believed that the next game—the next practice—would be his big chance. Sometimes, that faith made me cry myself to sleep at night. If only he could play the infield just once, I thought, it would make him so happy.

But Ford never got that chance. He displayed the generic at-least-you-participated trophy on the special shelf in his bedroom anyway.

"Next year," he told me, "when all the big kids have moved up a league, I'll be the oldest player and maybe I'll get to play first base."

"Yes, maybe," I said.

"Next year" came last week. On our way to the first practice of the season, I looked in my rearview mirror and saw Ford smiling to himself, staring confidently out the window. His baseball glove was in his lap. I knew he was daydreaming about playing the infield. With the same faith that one knows the daffodils will bloom each Spring, Ford believed that this day would be his big break.

In the parking lot, he jumped out of the car and ran across the dusty field, calling out "See ya mom," over his shoulder. He was too excited to wait for me to unbuckle his brother and put the baby in the stroller. My eyes grew wet when I noticed that his grey baseball pants, the ones that needed a belt and hung down to his ankles last year, now almost looked too tight and short as he ran to the field. Maybe this will be his big day after all, I thought.

I took my seat on the splintered stands and said a little prayer before the practice began. The sparkles in Ford's eyes nearly danced, and he couldn't contain the smile on his face as the new coach introduced himself to the team. Then the coach split the children into two groups. One group went to practice in the infield. The other group went to the outfield. Ford was in the second group. I could not stop myself from crying, and I hoped that the other mothers didn't see. While he fielded grounders and caught pop-fly's, Ford constantly glanced longingly at the kids in the infield. Perhaps, like me, he thought the coach would switch the groups halfway through practice. But we were both wrong. One hour passed, and Ford was still in the outfield.

When he came to me on the stands after practice, Ford said, "I really thought I'd be in the infield this year."

"I know, Honey," was all I could say. What else was there? I was prepared for him to say that he wanted to quit.

"I'm going to go talk to the coach," Ford said.

Uh-oh.

He ran across the dirt and waited for the coach to finish picking up stray balls and baseball bats. I turned in my seat and whistled at the wind, pretending not to know the precocious little boy about to confront his coach.

"Coach, I've been practicing real hard all summer," Ford said. "And if you just give me one shot at the infield, I think I can do it."

The coach smiled and tousled Ford's hair. "Sure, we'll give you a shot next practice," he said.

Ford ran back to me yelling, "Yes! He said he'd give me a chance, Mom!"

All weekend, Ford practiced in the front yard. He studied Major League games on television. And when Monday night's practice finally arrived, there he was in my rearview mirror again, smiling out the window.

He ran out onto the baseball field and the coach put him on first base. I have never smiled so much. There was my child, standing in a cloud of red baseball dust, his hands on his knees, ready for whatever came his way. He caught some and missed others, but he was there, and I knew he would remember that moment for the rest of his life.

After practice, Ford told me, "I'm glad they gave me a chance, because without a chance, how can anybody ever know what someone can do?"

It occurred to me that with his patience, his faith and determination, Ford will be able to do absolutely anything. And I hope he always has the chance.

Not An Easy Out

From previous columns, you have probably gathered that I'm a little sensitive when it comes to my boys' athletics. But just in case you had any doubt, I proved it to a crowd of about twenty adult onlookers last night.

Physical talents have not come easily to my oldest son, Ford, 7. It has taken practice, prayer and good luck just to get him on first base. I'm not exaggerating when I say that in his first season of tee-ball, the only reason Ford ever made it to any base was through the other team's errors. "I can't believe he made it," was a common sentiment from the stands.

But Ford never gave up, not even when he missed balls his younger brother, Owen, could catch, or when he tripped over air running to Second. At the beginning of this current season, his second playing tee-ball, Ford petitioned the coach to let him play the infield. "Coach, I've been practicing real hard all summer," he said. "If you just give me one shot at the infield, I think I can do it." The coach put him at second base and has delighted with us in Ford's determination and spirit ever since.

So you can imagine my shock when Ford was up at bat last night and the other team's coach yelled to his players, "This one's an easy out, guys." He said it three more times—"Easy out, guys. Easy out."—which was bad enough, but what was actually worse, ironically, was that Ford didn't seem to hear it. No, he was smiling up at me and his dad in the stands. "Hey, look at me," his eyes were saying. "Aren't you proud of me? Watch me hit this ball, Mom and Dad!"

Let me stop here and remind you that this is tee-ball, not the Major Leagues, not even high-school baseball. I think yelling discouraging comments about any 6- or 7-year-old who is learning a new sport is similar to a kindergarten teacher saying to her class, "This kid is stupid; this kid can't read!" Degrading remarks don't belong on the tee-ball field any more than they belong in the classroom. And yet, somehow, they are frequently tolerated at the former even if not in the latter.

When I look back on this moment now, it's as if everything was in slow motion. The coach's words escaped from his mouth in one long, dreadful sound: "Eaaaasssyyyyy ooooouuuut." I could feel the part of me that doesn't back down rising up. It's the part of me that staged a sit-in at the Ford dealership when I was seven-months pregnant because the manager wouldn't replace our Firestone tires. It's the part of me that stood up to our homebuilder, even when he threatened me with his tractor, and later testified against him at his trial. It's the part of me that perhaps should have been a lawyer, if not Bill O'Reilly's intern.

After the game was over, I went to the other coach and asked to talk to him about what he had said. Ten minutes later, the coach was yelling at me, I was crying, and Dustin was pretending not to know me because he avoids confrontation at all costs.

I turned to one of the loudest mothers on our team for backup. She's the one who once threatened to throw a pencil at an official for making a bad call. If Dustin wouldn't support me, I knew she would. Yet her expression was all "stinks to be you, Sarah." Later she said, "I'm all talk, Sarah. I don't usually confront people, and especially not people like that coach."

All information I could have used two days ago.

Finally I walked away from the coach because I realized there's no reasoning with a grown man who delights in 6- and 7-year-olds winning or losing at tee-ball as if it were the World Series. But there was still this little issue of my pride.

"I feel like I made a fool of myself," I told Dustin once we were in the car.

"No, the coach made a fool of himself," Dustin said.

"And why did you just stand there?" I asked.

"Because I knew you could handle it."

Imagine that. My Navy pilot husband—the one trained for combat—thinks I can "handle it."

And then a little voice came from the back of the car. "I'm glad you stuck up for me, Mom," Ford said. "But really it's OK. I heard what the coach said, but it didn't bother me because I knew I'd prove him wrong. I'm not an easy out."

Neither am I, Ford. Neither am I.

The Back-To-School Questionnaire

It is now back-to-school season, which only means that parents are filling out stacks of paperwork. It's quite overwhelming really. There are blue cards, yellow cards, shot records, and Superman lunch boxes to be found. There is glue to buy, new clothes to wash, and an empty shoe box/craft donation for the teacher. I don't think I was as prepared for my first year of college.

This fall, Ford will go to preschool full-time. Just yesterday, we began the process of getting ready. As Mom, my first task was to find shot records that have been missing since our last military move. I was also, unfortunately, responsible for hunting down a Spiderman action figure who "walks with his feet"—the kind that Ford's friend Max has. Because who knows what would happen if Ford started the new school year without a Spiderman who walks on his feet.

I was doing alright with most of this, until the new teacher sent an about-your-child questionnaire for me to complete and return.

One of the first questions on the form was, "Does your child tire easily?" I looked up from my place at the kitchen table and saw Ford leaping through the air, arms outstretched and yelling "SUPERMAAAAN!"

I looked back at the form, smiled and wrote, "Unfortunately, No."

Question: What is his/her request words for using the bathroom?

They are supposed to ask? Should I not admit that Ford is fond of urinating outside?

Question: Does your child have any problems we should know about?

Define "problem," I thought. Is calling himself Superman and dressing up in a red cape every single day considered a real problem?

Question: Does your child have any allergies?

Ah, an easy one.

Answer: Yes, he's highly allergic to Kryptonite. Don't worry, he'll explain.

Question: What type of discipline works best with your child?
Answer: If you find one, please let us know.
Question: What holds your child's attention the longest?
Answer: (Blank)
I was zipping through the questionnaire, until I got to this:
"Father's Work Information"

As a military BRAT myself, I have always dreaded this part of school forms. My dad's work address was a series of acronyms the teacher didn't understand. If he ever had a "work phone number," I didn't know it, because it probably changed as often as he deployed and came home.

This is the section that truly rubs salt in many military kids' wounds. Yes, your parents are still together, but no, they don't live at the same address. Yes, your dad is employed, but no, you don't know exactly where. Yes, you really do have a dad, but no, the teacher might not ever meet him.

I filled out "Dad's Work Information" as best I could.

Address: NAS something-or-other.

Then I came to the toughest part of all: "Describe your child."

This is a no-win situation for parents. Obviously, I think Ford is one (his younger brother Owen being the other) of the smartest, cutest and funniest kids on the planet, but do I really want to become one of "those parents." I pictured this teacher rolling her eyes at yet another student who will be "brilliant and polite," who "read when he was two-years old and can already do simple algebra."

We're still working on tying shoes and not burping at the dinner table. Ford can't read or count to 20, and this is exactly why he's going to school.

So how was I to answer this question? Do I tell the teacher that Ford talks too much and too loud, and that his nickname in last year's Thanksgiving play was "Chief-Talks-A-lot"? Do I tell her that he sits still for maybe two minutes out of every day?

No, no, no. Admitting to all this would set him up to be the "loud kid" in the class.

So what did I write?

Answer: Just call him Superman, and you'll be good friends.

Kindergarten Is Harder The Second Time

From worrying about who to sit with on the school bus to fretting over spilled milk in the cafeteria, it only took my son Ford, 5, one week and he was fully immersed in the American experience that is elementary school. Therefore, as his mother, so was I.

Kindergarten was hard the first time around. It's even harder the second time.

Ford wasn't excited about kindergarten. In fact, his first words coming off the bus were, "I hate it, and I'm never going back." I couldn't blame him. In fact, I sympathized. There's something about sending your child off to kindergarten that evokes both fear and empathy in any parent who's also been to public school.

When I helped Ford onto the bus that first morning, I was overwhelmed by one thing in particular: the peculiar smell (oily vinyl seats mixed with diesel fuel) of school buses hasn't changed in twenty years. Ford stood on the top step while I took pictures. He had a frozen, bewildered look on his face that mothers everywhere recognize. It's the I-think-I'm-going-to-be-sick look.

Ford slid into the first seat behind the driver and hugged his new dinosaur backpack to his chest. Right then, I wanted to grab him in my arms and say, "OK, fine, I'll homeschool you!" But Ford and I both know that would never work. I'm not disciplined enough to take full responsibility for my child's education. Actually, it was Ford who this summer said, "I don't want to ride the bus to school, but if Mom drives me, she'll make me late." So I swallowed back the lump in my throat and told Ford, "Why don't you go to the back of the bus? I bet your friends from the neighborhood are there." I peered back toward the last seats but saw no heads at all, just a few wispy hairs sticking up from the heads of children who aren't tall enough to see over the backs of seats. "They're just babies!" I thought, debating again whether or not I should take Ford home and never let him out of my sight.

But Ford took my suggestion and left his spot to sit at the back of the bus. Just then, two bigger kids looked down the aisle from near the back row, and I knew, regrettably, what I had done. I had sent my child into the lion's den. I rode a school bus for ten years; I should have known that "the back of the bus" is no place for a scared kindergartner with his socks pulled up to his knees.

As the bus pulled away, Ford looked out the window, and I could see that he was starting to cry. I would have chased the bus and brought him home, except I was wearing a long pink robe and pajamas underneath.

I called my mom as soon as I got back to the house.

"Remember how scared you were on the first day of kindergarten?" she said. "You wouldn't even go in the classroom. I thought you never would."

"So how did you get me to do it?" I asked.

"I told you, 'It's a law that you have to go to school, and if you don't, Mommy will go to jail'."

"My gosh, that's awful!" I said. "No wonder I never liked school. I can't believe you said that to me. Couldn't you come up with something a little more reassuring?"

"I didn't know what else to do," she said. "I was scared that you might never go into the classroom without crying first, and I couldn't deal with that heartache every morning."

I spent the next six hours pacing through the house, chewing my nails. Would Ford like school? Would he come home happy? Were the big kids on the bus nice to him? Or would I have to track them down and tie their shoestrings together?

At 2:45 in the afternoon, Ford's bus rumbled down the street. I stood on the driveway. I could see his big brown eyes staring out the window. I held my breath when the doors opened.

"I hate it, and I'm never going back," he said. Then he started to cry. "I want to stay home. I want you to teach me at home. I never want to ride the bus again."

Children

I was scared—frantic, even. My heart felt pulled in all directions, crying along with my young son. I was speechless, and ... well, desperate.

So I said the only thing I could think of. "You have to go back, Honey, because it's the law, and Mommy will go to jail if you don't."

An Evening In Jail
With The Cub Scouts

Before I explain why I spent the evening at the county jail, let me first tell you how Dustin became den leader for our son Ford's Cub Scout group. Ford, who can spell words like "democracy" and adds multiple numbers in his head faster than his mother can, isn't afraid of many things except for:

the dark,

bears,

and sleeping outside in the dark, with bears.

Rather than signing up for something a little more congruent with his personality—something like the Young Republicans or the Science Club—Ford decided to try scouting. No one was more shocked than his dad and me.

At the local scouting store, however, where we spent what seemed like Ford's college savings on a Cub Scout uniform, badges and other paraphernalia, I began to understand Ford's desire to be a Tiger Cub. He wanted to wear that blue uniform in the worst way. Dustin would not realize this insight until I told him later. So, with a bundle of equipment in his arms, he looked down at Ford and said, "Won't it be fun when we go camping together?" The blood drained from Ford's face. "You mean this will involve caaaaamping?" he said. "With bears? In the dark?"

To help ease Ford's anxiety, Dustin, the Navy pilot trained for war, volunteered to be den leader along with our neighbor, Dan, a Marine pilot trained for war. Ford may be afraid of camping, but Dustin is decidedly more afraid of organizing crafts and folksy sing-alongs. He could probably handle himself sleeping in the dark with bears, but we both knew he might glue his thumb to his knee if left to figure out paper mache on his own. Therefore, I became a "silent" den leader, ready to step in whenever the glue sticks and construction paper became too much.

Last week, however, due to other obligations, I was unable to assist when it was Dustin's turn to set up the weekly den outing. The boys were going to see a police station, but when the sheriff called to confirm, he said, "Your tour of the county jail is all set up. We'll see you Tuesday night."

The county jail? Did Dustin really set up a tour of the jail for a group of 6- and 7-year-olds? I wondered. Surely there is some mistake!

But no, there was no mistake. Tuesday night, on the way to the jail, Ford started to cry. "Will we see prisoners?" he asked.

"Of course not," I said. "They won't take you back with the prisoners. They'll probably show you where they keep the police cars, and maybe they have a pretend jail cell set up for display."

Inside the jail lobby, a sergeant gave us our instructions:

"Keep you hands in your pockets at all times. Do not touch anything, especially not the doors. Don't look the prisoners in the eyes. Do not speak to them. Remember, these are very dangerous individuals."

I'm not sure whose eyes looked more afraid, the children's or their mothers'.

"You will never live this down," I whispered to Dustin.

Our first stop on the tour: watching two new inmates as they were escorted from a police car to the "intake" room. Second stop: seeing a dozen male criminals confined to a room together, waiting for their cell. Third stop: the restraining chair, where rowdy inmates are strapped down at their ankles, wrists, and, if necessary, their head. "Anyone want to test it out?" the sergeant asked. Ford did not raise his hand.

The sergeant had already told us that the jail has two types of inmates. Those in the blue suits are "your average criminal." The ones in the red suits are the "really, really bad guys." When he said our fourth stop would be the jail cell, where we would see actual prisoners, Ford clutched my hand.

"Don't worry, I'm sure it will just be the blue-suit people. They wouldn't take you to see the red suits," I whispered to him.

"When you see the guys in the red suits in here, remember, don't make eye contact," the sergeant said.

There was no way to make the situation better. In Ford's short time as a Cub Scout, he has managed to get out of every camping event. So I leaned down and told him, "Maybe scouting doesn't always involve camping, but I honestly didn't know it would mean seeing prisoners."

Although, I guess, that's what you get when your den leaders are a Navy pilot and a Marine.

I'm Just Saying…

The Military

The Military:

It's Fabio Underpants Naked.

Things You Should Know About Military Men

Q: When my husband says we will leave for our summer vacation at "zero-six-hundred hours," what does that mean exactly?

A: It means you will pile into the minivan at an ungodly hour, and that your husband needs to chill.

This scenario is so typical of military men, who in their professional lives operate within the confines of rigid procedures and schedules. When they get home, they like to think that their families also tense at the sound of a whistle and meet the day with gusto. Yet it is one of life's cruel ironies that military men often (not always, but often) coexist with their opposite: a woman who doesn't wear a watch and likes to sleep in; children who take an hour to get on their shoes, use the bathroom one last time, find a toy to take along, use the bathroom again, find the toy they set down, get one last sip of juice, use the bathroom one more time and get out the door.

Ah, but military men are also great planners and strategists, so my guess is that your husband really wants to leave at 7:00 a.m. (aka: "zero-seven-hundred"), but he knows this is unrealistic. He has told you 6:00 a.m. in the hopes that the family will actually be in the car one hour later. All of which means you won't get the "you-guys-are-so-undisciplined" stare until about 7:05, so take your time.

Q: Why can my husband fly million-dollar aircraft but for the past nine months, he hasn't figured out how to fix the broken sprinkler in our front yard?

A: First, I'm impressed that you realize your husband's procrastination with the sprinkler has more to do with his inability to fix it than any restraints on his time. A less experienced military wife might be fooled into believing that her husband has been "too busy" to think about the sprinkler. But we know (because we are the ones who do all the home repairs most of the time anyway) that a broken sprinkler requires very little time or skill.

However, as you mentioned, your husband is a highly trained military man. (Which is to say, if the military didn't teach it, he probably doesn't know it.) You are witnessing a very common phenomenon: Smart people don't have room left in their brains for mundane tasks such as remembering to turn off the stove, storing new contacts into their cell phone, and reprogramming TiVo. Basically, your husband has used up all his smarts on the military. So get out there, fix that sprinkler, and be done with it!

Q: When I met my soldier husband, I fell in love with the idea that he would be my protector. Then he deployed, and I had to toughen up. I hate to say it, but sometimes he seems a little wimpy to me now. Is this normal?
A: Military marriages are delicate balancing acts. When your husband is deployed, you are on your own, and you rise to the occasion. Then he comes back and naturally wants your relationship to return to its previous state (that, of course, being with you as the "wife" and him as the "soldier husband," while "Up Where We Belong" plays softly, yet continuously, in the background). As you gain independence, it is a bit disconcerting to view your husband in a different light. Trust me when I say you will not only get used to it, eventually you will enjoy telling everyone that your husband moaned like a baby when he had Pink Eye, even after you've delivered three of his children. Not that I know a couple this has happened to, but you get the idea.

Q: Who are Romeo, Charlie and Sierra, and why does my husband keep talking about them?
A: Being the efficient system it is, the military uses the phonetic alphabet to eliminate any confusion (between Bs, Ds, Ts and Vs, and so forth) when calling out letters. For instance, my initials are SRS. To my military husband this is "Sierra Romeo Sierra." You can learn the phonetic alphabet if you wish, but I prefer instead to irritate my

husband by coming up with my own. Instead of spelling out my husband's name Delta-Uniform-Sierra-Tango-India-November (the correct way), I might use Donkey-Umbrella-Salad-Tutu-Igloo-Norway. This is only slightly less efficient but much more Fabio-Underpants-Naked.

A Lesson In Military Speak

Sea bag. Spouse Club. Duty. DITY. Det.

If this looks like Greek to you, you're not alone. Deciphering the strange and confusing language of the military takes time and patience. To make life easier, here's a brief crash-course lesson in military terminology.

Let's start with "sea bag." Ask your spouse and he will probably tell you that this is a standard-issued bag used by military personnel to transport clothes and uniforms. And he is correct. Well, almost. For the sake of clarity, I like to describe the sea bag as the deployment time capsule a husband brings home and dumps on the living room floor. Open the bag and you will find undershirts that are smelly, wrinkled and gray (even though you could swear they were fresh and white when he packed them six months ago), and an assortment of gifts—knick-knacks and tacky clothing in all the wrong sizes—lovingly handpicked for you in a foreign port. (I've heard tales about women opening the sea bag and finding lavish jewelry, but so far this is just a myth to me.)

Now let's tackle DITY. DITY is an acronym for a "do-it-yourself" move, which technically means you pack and move your belongings without the aid of a moving company. You will recognize the DITY move when your husband asks, "Honey, can you spend the next two weeks sorting through all of our belongings and begging the grocery store for boxes while I cleverly and conveniently disappear to finish up my important check-out procedure on base?"

Which brings us to the word "duty." The word seems straightforward and simple enough: a position of watch filled at regulated intervals by military personnel. And this is what your spouse will want you to believe. After all, he believes it! Soon you will learn, however, that duty is actually an unavoidable work commitment that pops up unexpectedly on weekends, anniversaries, holidays, and your son's first day of school. How these scheduled duty shifts always sneak up and surprise my husband, I do not know.

The title CO is an especially important acronym to learn. This stands for commanding officer, and he/she is your husband's boss—the head honcho. In front of the CO, it is advisable to refrain from calling your spouse "pooky" or "bear," or to mention that he threw-up on his first T-34 flight.

Another common abbreviation used in the military is det (aka: detachment). This, your husband will tell you, is a scheduled, brief period of time during which his unit or squadron leaves the home base for training.

Don't be fooled.

Look for the meaning of det under its more common name: "impossible unpredictability." When your husband claims to have a det in one week that will last "only five days," be prepared that he will probably actually leave tomorrow and be gone for two weeks. Never trust the det schedule, and be leery of anyone who claims to know the det schedule.

And finally, there is the Spouse Club. Your husband might refer to this group as the official military "rumor mill." The Spouse Club, however, is an essential refuge from loneliness when your husband is deployed, and then a reasonable excuse to escape from too much together-time when he gets back. The Spouse Club also is an excellent source of information (such as why the squadron really calls your husband "Dancing Bear"), and a means to clarify facts (like the truth behind that questionable picture of your husband in Greece). WARNING: Anything you reveal at a Spouse Club meeting may be used against you. Use discretion.

Husbands and wives have been arguing for years over the meaning of most of these words. For the most part, his definition and your perception will eventually differ greatly.

There is one exception, however, and that is the word "orders." Husbands and wives unanimously agree about the cut-and-dried nature of this word. "Orders," unfortunately, means exactly what you think it means: Your spouse is being ordered to do something. It will often be used in sentences like, "Yes, honey, I thought we'd be moving to Virginia, too, but now I'm being ordered to Japan," and

"My orders have changed, we're moving next week."

There's just no getting around orders, no matter how you define the word.

Good luck, stay flexible, and don't believe everything you hear. Especially about the det schedule.

Military Terms Unclassified

From time to time, readers catch me using a seemingly outdated, inappropriate or misplaced word, such as when I call an aircraft carrier a "boat" and a deployment "cruise." Much of the discrepancies in language can be blamed on my upbringing. There are surprising differences between the communities of the military, and because my father was a Navy pilot, I grew up hearing, for instance, that even a 1,094-ft. aircraft carrier looks like a "boat" when you're about to land on it.

Furthermore, military terminology varies depending on which side of the fence you stand. As a military child and wife, I feel at liberty to call six-month deployments "cruises." But if my hairdresser, dentist, or paperboy asks about my husband's "cruise," I'm likely to think, "What do they think this is, the 'Love Boat'?"

So when I say "boat" or "cruise," when I should say "ship" and "deployment," it is out of affection and, yes, ignorance because I was raised and married into a specific community with it's own lingo.

However, all this is not to say that there are not blatant errors in some of the military's official definitions. I know this because finicky readers who pick up on my misnomers sometimes send me instruction books or photocopied handouts to enlighten my military vernacular. (Yes, there are people who own such things.)

I am certain that you, like me, will be amazed at some of the mistakes these supposed guides have made. After all this time, you'd think the military would have it figured out. Nevertheless, here are just a few of the most glaring incorrect definitions that I've come across.

DISPLACEMENT

Military Definition: The weight of water displaced by the ship, equal to the weight of the ship.

Correction: Being moved across country on short notice, only to learn you will move back again after your husband's six-month training stint.

FENDER

Military Definition: Device used to take the shock of contact between ship and pier.

Correction: What I dented backing into the trash can the day after my husband left for deployment.

FLARE

Military Definition: Pyrotechnic signal used to attract attention.

Correction: What happens to my blood pressure during the witching hour (5:00–6:00 p.m.) when my husband is working late and the kids are swinging light sabers at each other in the living room.

LIFELINE

Military Definition: The lines erected around the edge of the deck of a ship.

Correction: My buddies in the Spouse Club.

NIGHT VISION

Military Definition: The ability to see at night.

Correction: The ability to perceive exactly what time your husband stumbled into the bedroom after a night out with the guys.

THIMBLE

Military Definition: Metal ring that fits inside an eye splice.

Correction: A cap used to protect your thumb when sewing. Duh.

WALK AWAY

Military Definition: To haul a line by taking hold and walking down the deck.

Correction: What my husband should do after he tells me we are moving again in two months.

BORE
Military Definition: The interior diameter of the barrel of a gun.
Correction: Listening to my husband recite his emergency procedures.

COMMANDING OFFICER
Military Definition: An officer in charge of a unit, base, station, ship, etc.
Correction: Mom.

CLASSIFIED INFORMATION
Military Definition: Sensitive information that requires protection for national security.
Correction: All the things that Mom let the kids do while Dad was at sea.

BAIL
Military Definition: To remove water from a ship.
Correction: What the ship/squadron usually does when a hurricane is on its way.

BRIGHTWORK
Military Definition: Metal that is kept polished.
Correction: Taking your kids to the wrong restaurant for their birthday party.

DEAD IN THE WATER
Military Definition: A ship that is stopped and can not go on.
Correction: How your husband will feel when you're not buying his excuse for coming home with glitter on his face.

ANCHOR
Military Definition: Used to make a floating body stay fast to the bottom.
Correction: What a military spouse is to his/her family, not just during deployment, but every day.

FAQs About Military Spouses

Often I receive emails from spouses asking for my advice. It amuses my husband, Dustin, that I—the woman who once stood in the post office and distractedly instructed her son, "stamps always go on the upper left side of the envelope, Honey," and then watched none the wiser as he licked and pressed postage on the wrong corner of fifty greeting cards—have become a source of education for hundreds of other women.

Nevertheless, for the record, I cannot respond to personal queries via email, so I have taken some of the most frequently asked questions and answered them here. Take my advice for what it's worth ... about as much as a soggy, used postage stamp.

Question: I just moved to a new duty station and no one from the Spouse Club has contacted me yet. I'm beginning to feel left out. Should I take it personally?
Answer: Most likely your existence is caught up in military-spouse bureaucracy. There is a system for getting your contact information to the correct person, and it goes something like this: Your spouse checks into their command. The command asks, "Are you married?" The command alerts the Spouse Club. The Spouse Club tags the Hospitality Chair. The Hospitality Chair places a friendly telephone call to welcome you to the group.

Theoretically this system is fool proof. Then again, theoretically men should always come home on time and not say things like, "My socks with the holes in them are my favorite." So on second thought, your predicament is probably due to the fact that your spouse forgot your new address and phone number when he was checking in. Or when the CO asked, "Are you married?" your spouse said, "No." If the latter is true, you have my blessing to throw out his socks with the holes.

Question: What should I wear to my first Spouse Club meeting?
Answer: Forget what you've heard about gloves and not wearing white after Labor Day. There's just one rule of thumb when choosing what to wear for a Spouse Club event: Don't be the only spouse in costume. So long as you know that a "Southern Living" party isn't a chance to drag out your Scarlett O'Hara hoop skirt, be yourself and wear whatever you like.

Question: Should I call the commanding officer's (CO's) wife "Mrs."?
Answer: Yes and no. Common niceties such as "please," "thank you," and "ma'am" aside, military spouses don't have a rank and don't require formal titles. The CO's wife isn't your boss. If she acts like she is, you have the option to talk behind her back or find another support group. I suggest the latter.

Question: Once a month I leave my husband with the kids and go to the local Spouse Club meeting. Only, these "meetings" seem more like parties, and I sort of look forward to them. Shouldn't I feel guilty for sticking my husband with kid duty while I'm having so much fun?
Answer: No. If ever you are tempted to feel guilty, repeat the following: "I bathed and diapered the children for six months while he was at sea. I can't keep a career because we move every three years. I pull apart my husband's nasty, used handkerchiefs each time I put them in the washing machine. My husband is lucky I'm coming home at all."

Question: I think there are a few women in my Spouse Club who don't like me. Shouldn't we all love and support each other?
Answer: Take note of others in the animal kingdom at your local zoo. Some species of females can't even be kept in the same enclosure or else they will maul each other. Female lemurs, in particular, are known for being extremely hostile toward unfamiliar "girlfriends." Whoever decided that human females could break the

phenomenon of female-female aggression in the animal world must have been a man.

Question: After all of this, do you still think people should join the Spouse Club? Is it really worth it?

Answer: Absolutely! Trust me, I wouldn't lead you astray on this. Just don't ask me to stamp your envelopes.

Etiquette
For Your Next Holiday Party

Dear Sarah, I'm nervous about the upcoming holiday party for my husband's unit. Is there anything I should know about etiquette before I go?

Presumably, you have read *Service Etiquette*, because we (ahem) all have. If this is the case, disregard most of what you read. Nothing against *Service Etiquette*, except that much like raising children, it is easier to read about military etiquette than to actually put it into practice.

If this is your first military social event, you might have visions of women in white gloves passing out their calling cards to all the young wives. But have you seen any such women at the commissary? At the exchange/PX? These women only exist in people's fantasies (or nightmares) about military life. (Which isn't to say that some scary things aren't going to happen at the party, but we'll get to that in a minute.) The men and women you will meet at the holiday party will be the same men and women you have met at your husband's place of work, that you've run into at the mall, or that you've seen bowling with their children at the base alley. Don't assume that just because it is an official event (aka, "forced fun," or "a highly encouraged social outing") that your husband's co-workers and their spouses will suddenly morph into *Service Etiquette*-beaters. The truth is that only some of them will. These are the people you will avoid.

The only real concern you should have at the holiday party is what to say, when and to whom. For instance, the flight surgeon, or any other person associated with your spouse's healthcare for that matter, is not the person to which you should tell your story about the black spot your husband sometimes sees when he looks up at a blue sky. Pilots especially are funny about their health. (And by "funny" I mean that they would rather you tell the flight surgeon about the stuffed bear named "Pooh" that their mother still keeps on their bed at home than they would for you to tell them about the twitch they sometimes get in their left eyelid.) As far as his co-workers at the party are concerned, your husband is the picture of health. He doesn't even snore, and he certainly doesn't sleepwalk. (Feel free to laugh about these things with the other wives in the bathroom, however.)

Another situation that might come up involves gifts and/or door prizes. The more rank your husband attains, the more he will insist that you not accept any door prizes. "Just tell them to call another ticket," he might say. However, let me advise you from personal experience that he does not mean for you to refuse any door prizes that are free tickets to a major football game. You are to refuse everything except those items that your husband personally covets.

You might also be concerned about what to call your spouse's superiors. Do you call them Sir? Commander so-and-so? Will you look like a suck-up if you do? Will you look like a slacker if you don't? A general rule of thumb is to call them whatever you feel most comfortable calling them. Unless, of course, your husband will pay for it at work on Monday. For instance, some communities call the commanding officer's wife a COW (get it; commanding officer's wife?), but I wouldn't use this term of endearment until it is abundantly clear that the commanding officer's wife and her husband know about the tradition.

Alcohol could be an issue, too. Your goal is to not be the drunkest spouse at the party. People will always talk about the drunkest spouse. Don't let this be you. Also, use caution if there will be music and/or dancing at the party. You never want to be the first or last spouse out on the dance floor. If you heed my warning about alcohol, this shouldn't be a problem. If you feel compelled to dance, just make sure you aren't the only one doing the Funky Chicken, the Macarena, or any other type of line dance.

Basically, when I think about how best to advise you, I am

reminded of my eleven-month-old son. Lindell knows how to clap, and sometimes he can wave bye-bye and point. But when all else fails, he simply claps and smiles. That is his default trick. Always have a safe, default behavior, and let it not involve abundant amounts of alcohol, any "funky" dance, or stories about your husband's hemorrhoids.

Some Of These People Have Seen Me Naked

According to the commanding officer (CO) at Naval Hospital Pensacola, the first thing the outgoing CO and the public affairs officer briefed him on before taking command was yours truly. They even gave him copies of all my columns regarding the hospital. Gosh, if I had known that, I would have written more.

In any case, I became aware of this little gem when I had the honor of speaking at the Navy Medical Ball last week.

Imagine my surprise when I received the invitation. After some of the things I've written about military medicine, I never suspected the CO would want to see me at all, unless it was to set me straight. In his remarks at the ball, however, the CO referred to me as a discerning critic with a "keen eye," someone who reminds them of the "human side" of medicine. (My husband just calls me a pain, but OK.) I take this is as an encouraging sign that the hospital is listening, that they aren't oblivious to their problems. They are receptive to hearing about their strengths *and* their weaknesses.

In other words, they're working on it.

As the meal was served, I watched the doctors and nurses carefully. "Just eat what they eat," I whispered to Dustin. "Because, you know, they are the health experts and all."

But Dustin was not about to pass up the opportunity to eat a big slab of red, artery-clogging meat. And besides, he was decidedly more concerned about the presence of NOMI (Naval Operational Medicine Institute). These guys are the first gatekeepers of Naval Aviation. They have the power to find a new career path for any pilot who doesn't match the Navy's physical requirements. I instinctively knew that the NOMI folks should not hear my story about Dustin getting sick all over a T-34.

As I stood at the podium to give my speech, I felt the usual, healthy rush of stage fright that befalls most public speakers. I tried the age-old tactic of picturing my audience naked. Then it occurred to me that a disconcerting amount of the audience had seen me waiting in a cold room wearing nothing but a paper gown and my socks. Some of them, in fact, had seen my insides on an ultrasound. Talk about knowing your audience and vice versa.

When I was done, the event's planning committee chair presented me with a beautifully engraved pen and her wish that I give the hospital only good press in the future (don't worry guys, I'm always honest, but fair). Then the CO gave me a handsome coin with the hospital's emblem on it. I asked him if this is my new key to appointments whenever I want them and quicker service at Immunizations. Alas, the military is nothing if not by the rules; I will wait like everyone else.

With that, the formal portion of the night concluded and the dancing began. This is when I saw some of my doctors doing the Electric Slide. Yes, the Electric Slide. I realized then that miscommunication between the military hospital and its patients is a two-way street. While I've opined that doctors and nurses sometimes forget that we are humans and not just the "last four" of our sponsor's Social Security number, perhaps I've missed that my doctors and nurses are human, too. Deep, I know. Just when you got over the shock that your kindergarten teacher didn't live at the school, I come in and tell you that the man or woman overseeing your blood pressure and cholesterol is not only human, but might possibly know the Macarena, too.

Ah, but the enlightenment doesn't stop there. The DJ (to be discussed in next week's column because the story is so good it needs its own space) had more dance music up his sleeve, and so the learning continued. I met our pediatrician's wife and discovered that she is much more fun than I might have imagined. The doctor had another dimension: a wife with a super-cute haircut who told me stories of their early days as parents. I also saw one of our doctors talking and laughing with a pathologist (yes, pathologists can laugh).

Still, the biggest surprise of the night was the DJ, and for that you'll have to wait for another column.

And Others Have Seen Me In My Wonder Woman Bikini

As mentioned previously, I was the guest speaker at Naval Hospital Pensacola's medical ball in May. The Navy is an awfully small world, and I knew chances were good that I would run into someone I know. My fear, however, was that this familiar someone would be a gynecologist or a labor and delivery nurse, someone who has seen a little too much of me. It never crossed my mind that the disc jockey (DJ) might possibly be someone who has seen me in a Wonder Woman bathing suit.

At the ball, I was seated next to the hospital's commanding officer (CO). I was telling him that my dad is a retired F-14 pilot, and he said, "the DJ's father is also an old F-14 guy."

If the Navy is a small world, the F-14 community is even smaller. It's like a village. Or maybe like the Naval Academy: anyone who's ever flown an F-14 most likely knows everyone else who has as well.

"What's the DJ's last name?" I asked, quite sure that I would know it. When the CO answered, there was a familiarity there, like the smell of antiques at my parents' house, or the way our front door squeaks when it opens. In fact, I knew I had seen the DJ's last name on dozens of Christmas cards throughout the years. It was one of those names that I had heard over and over again when my parents retold stories. At the moment, I couldn't recall the DJ's first name, or even his parents' names, but I knew that the last name was part of my family's vernacular.

Way back when, "Smiley" was one of those familiar names as well, because Dustin's dad and my dad were in the same squadron (VF-

111) at NAS Miramar in San Diego, Calif., when I was born. Yes, I have known my husband since I was a baby. Our moms were in the Spouse Club together for several years, but eventually the Navy pulled the Smileys and my family in different directions, and for almost a decade "Dustin" was a just a name on a yearly Christmas card. (Dustin and I didn't start dating until we were in our 20s.)

The DJ's last name was as familiar to me as "Smiley" used to be before it was my name. The CO continued talking, unaware of my moment of nostalgia, and then I blurted out, a little too loudly, "I know him!" The CO looked stunned. "I mean I don't really know him," I said. "But my parents know his parents. The DJ, I mean."

This all happened during dinner, and immediately afterwards, I was at the podium giving my speech. The DJ had no clue who I was, that we had a connection or that the CO and I had discussed him over baked chicken. I was so excited, however, that I forgot all this. Into the microphone I said, "I grew up in the military healthcare system. In fact, I grew up with the DJ." I glanced across the room and the look on the DJ's face was one that said, "Who the &#$* is this woman, and why did she just bring everyone's attention to me?"

I still couldn't place where I knew the DJ (as in, which squadron our dads shared), but I knew we had a history. I knew he had probably seen me in my Wonder Woman bathing suit back when I was a kid.

As it turns out, the DJ's dad was my dad's roommate on his first deployment onboard *USS Franklin Roosevelt*. It was the same deployment during which I was born; the same deployment I met Dustin; the same deployment Dustin's mom and my mom were in the Spouse Club together ... with the DJ's mom.

All our parents—all six of them—knew each other.

When I called my parents on the way home from the ball, I thought they'd be shocked to hear my news. I imagined (perhaps overly so) their surprise at having three grown kids from the same old squadron meeting serendipitously at a medical ball, of all things (since none of our dads were in the medical field).

But my parents just said, "Isn't that something! Neat!" because, yes, the military is really—and predictably—that small.

Santa Claus Might Be A Navy Pilot

Lately I've had suspicions that Santa Claus might be in the military. Indeed, I suspect he may be a Navy pilot. Beyond the obvious similarities—serving others, altruistic motivation, worldwide travel—between St. Nick and people in the military, there are other clues that point to Santa's real affiliation. So far, however, no one in or out of the military is spilling the beans—part of the "don't ask, don't tell" policy—so I've had to form the case on my own.

For 31 years I've believed Santa's whole I'm-just-a-civilian-living-in-the-North-Pole story, and frankly, the façade is wearing thin. I mean, barring the magical flying reindeer bit, can a man really travel the globe in just one night? Sounds like a lot of smoke and mirrors to me. And where do they teach the smoke-and-mirrors technique? Where else but in the military? ("Yes, Honey, while all the guys went to the nightclubs here in Spain, I went on a tour of the cathedrals." "I really hate that my training will be in Key West this weekend, but what can I do?" "Six months seems like a long time, but you'll be busy with the kids and it will go by quicker than you think.")

Yes, Santa is too good at the illusions to not be in the Navy. Believe what you will, but I think the evidence, especially the following, speaks for itself.

Santa has the easy part.

I think we all know who's behind the hard work of Christmas, and it isn't the man in a spiffy suit and shiny black boots. Santa gets all the glory while Mrs. Claus waits patiently at home and his elves do all the work. Does Mrs. Claus ever get to ride on the big magical sleigh? Does she travel the world? Do people leave cookies and milk for her? No, I didn't think so. And when was the last time Mrs. Claus got to spend a weekend in Key West and call it work. I mean … .

Also, what about those elves who build the toys, fix broken parts, and prepare the reindeer, only to have Santa swoop in at the last minute, jump into his aircraft—I mean, sleigh—then fly away to the applause and admiration of everyone who loves a man in uniform? I'd like to see what happens when Santa's sleigh has a hydraulic failure and there are no elves around to help him. Who's the hero then?

Santa's arrival inspires good behavior in children everywhere.

You hear it all the time in the aisles of Wal-Mart, mothers telling their children, "Remember that Santa is coming, and he doesn't want you to be naughty." But you can often hear nearly the same thing in military households: "Just wait until your father gets home! Do you want him to think you laid around on the couch for six months? Get out there and mow the lawn!" Yet the provoked good behavior is usually short lived in both instances. Reminders of Santa's arrival have little effect in March or April, as does the desire to make a good first impression at Dad's homecoming. Coincidence?

Recently, trying to catch my husband's co-workers at the squadron off guard, I asked, without warning or explanation, "Santa's really a Navy pilot, right?" But the guys didn't miss a beat. They weren't "telling." In fact, one pilot said he could tell me Santa's true identity, but then he'd have to kill me.

I tried and I pressed (Disclaimer: I never used torture), but these guys have been trained in resistance. All the pilots would concede to is reasons why Santa *should* be in the military:

"Nuclear power is more efficient than flying reindeer."

"The retirement benefits."

"Tax-free toys at the Exchange."

"He'd have a break from his wife for six months, not just one night."

"His elves would look better as sailors than in tights."

"When global warming (thanks Al Gore) melts the North Pole, Santa would have a boat to float on."

Sure, they made jokes, but it seemed to me that these Navy pilots know an awful lot about the jolly man in the red suit.

I'm just saying … .

Animals And Rocks (yes, rocks) Bothered By Jet Noise

Each day when Dustin goes to work and prepares to fly, he goes through a pre-flight checklist. First he checks the weather and notices to airmen. Then he conducts a flight brief and inspects the aircraft. But most importantly of all—if you're a cow, that is—he reviews maps for "noise sensitive areas." "Noise sensitive" areas are those places in which animals have complained about the level of noise pollution created by military aircraft.

Well, no, that's not quite true. The animals didn't complain. Their people did.

Apparently cows, horses, chickens, cats, and even fish exhibit odd behavior after repeated exposure to aircraft noise. Mainly, they stop mating and they lose weight, which don't sound like horrible side effects to me. But I'm not a horse.

Still, one night, after hearing a group of pilots complain about "too many 'noise sensitive' areas," I decided to do my own research as an unbiased, politically neutral individual. In other words, I only own one animal, a one-year-old border collie named Annie, and even though we live in an area heavily trafficked by military helicopters, the noise has never affected her desire to eat the knobs off our gas grill and to lick herself.

After a quick search on Google, it turns out that animals might have a valid complaint. According to the National Park Service's 2004 Sheep Report (I'm not kidding, that's the name of the report), "flight activity over wildlife [can] cause physiological and/or behavioral reactions that reduce the animals' fitness ... The way in which animals respond to overflights could interfere with raising young, habitat use, and physiological energy budgets." Whatever that means. The report went on to say that, "These costs could reduce reproductive success of individuals and lead to population declines."

Sounds very ominous.

However, another report, with the less ambiguous title, "Noise Effects on Wildlife," by the Noise Pollution Clearinghouse (use that for your next game of Balderdash) claims that overflights might cause animals to raise their heads and shift their bodies. That's right—military pilots across the country are causing our nation's wildlife to raise their heads and shift their bodies.

If you can even imagine abuse worse than that, the report also claims that more disturbed animals will "trot short distances" and "birds may walk around flapping their wings."

Sounds like a wedding party to me.

Lest you think animals are the only ones suffering from our military's practicing to protect the country, information from the Office of the Under Secretary of Defense claims that some people worry that our nation's rock formations are at risk as well. "Sometimes, inanimate objects can be sensitive to flight effects," the site reads. Apparently low-flying jets and helicopters can cause damage to "historic and cultural resources as well as rock formations."

But still, it is our animals and their people who have the gravest concerns. Cows run around their pastures. Birds needlessly flap their wings. Horses raise their heads. Bears shift their bodies. And animals everywhere stop eating and mating as aircraft pass overhead.

This is terrible news for the animal world, but might be somewhat encouraging for humans near air stations who complain about "jet noise." No need to feign a headache anymore, ladies. Simply tell your husband that your mating instincts are on hold so long as you're living in a flight pattern. And what could be an easier diet plan than listening to the rumble of jets and whop-whop of a helicopter?

Of course, if these two groups of complainers—the humans and the animals—truly do connect someday, if they meet to discuss their common vex over military aircraft noise, there's one thing certain to happen. Someday little gophers will protest outside the base. They'll find a poster-gopher who has lost hair and weight to prove their point. They'll write op-eds and lobby politicians.

If this does happen, my friends, we can only hope for one thing. Eventually some level-headed fish will stand on the opposite corner from his animal comrades, and he will hold up a sign that reads, "Jet noise is the sound of freedom."

Much Ado About Stickers

When I heard last month that the Air Force will soon eliminate its requirement that each military-family owned vehicle have a base decal, I was giddy with excitement. Finally, there would be reprieve from hours spent waiting in the PSD (Personnel Security Detachment) office for new stickers. No more fretting over which small square sticker goes on the left of the long rectangular one, and which sticker goes on the right. No more clinching teeth as I set the decal onto its final resting place, hoping that it is straight and correct. I imagined the possibilities of looking out my windshield and for once not being reminded of my husband's job, rank, last duty station, and the fact that our decals will soon expire. I envisioned washing the car windows and not worrying about the reflective stickers coming loose (lest I have to wait more hours at PSD for new ones), never mind that it takes a razor blade and lots of elbow grease to ultimately remove the decals. That's how scary the PSD office is; we will go to great, even foolish lengths, to avoid it.

And then I remembered that we are not Air Force. We are Navy. We will still have stickers.

Contrary to popular belief that base decals are for security, those rascally stickers actually got their start in the 1970s when they were created to manage traffic and basically create more hoops for vehicle registration. "Military wives aren't wasting enough time on base," one official might have said to another. "Let's make them register their vehicles now, too."

"But aren't their cars registered with the state already?" another official probably answered.

"Well, if you have a better suggestion for getting people to read old copies of *Retired Officer* in the lobby and to waste good money at the vending machines buying Sprite and M&M's for their kids, then let me know."

"You have a point. And just to make things even more frustrating, let's put a few grumpy civilian workers, the kind that can't be fired—not ever—behind the desk."

"Yes, and let's make each branch of service use a different database so that they cannot work together, and then, get this, even the base police will have hoops to jump through."

"Bwahahahaha."

There are, of course, many faults inherent to the base decal system. It's been a silly operation ever since laws began requiring that all motorists (civilian and military) have a state-issued driver's license, proof of registration and insurance, and an emissions and safety inspection before they can drive.

"We've been putting our own personnel through a process that simply duplicates state and federal mandatory requirements," Col. William Sellers, Air Force chief of force protection, said in a release put out by the Secretary of the Air Force Public Affairs.

What's more, base decals might even be a security concern because they single out military families, potentially making them a target for terrorists. Pre-9/11, it was common for base guards to permit vehicles on base simply because their decal was up-to-date and in the correct location. (Incidentally, it was also common for base guards to send yours truly straight to PSD because either my decal was expired or in the wrong position.) Post-9/11, however, I've never been admitted on base without someone checking my ID card first. Post-9/11, some military wives have actually scraped decals off their car to be more inconspicuous.

Yet for all its problems, I will miss base decals. Seeing them affixed to an oncoming car often causes me to nod and wave in a familiar way, like seeing another mom with a stroller full of kids at the mall. Base decals, especially the ones with eagles and stars on them, are also helpful in giving junior officers fair warning as to who they are about to cut off on the highway. And, of course, base decals offer us the chance to catch up on our reading at PSD.

Yes, I guess I'm becoming a bit emotional over the passing of this bastion of military life. I might even miss trips to PSD to wait in line ...

Oh, but wait. We're not Air Force. We're Navy.

So, um, save a copy of *Retired Officer* for me in the lobby.

The Military

Military Wives:

YES, WIVES.

The Military's Dirty Words

Did you know that "husband" and "wife" have become dirty little words in the military, replaced with the kinder, gentler "spouse"?

Yes, it's true. You can no longer say, "My husband is deployed." You have to say, "My spouse is deployed." And you're not a military wife. No way. You're a military *spouse*.

Political correctness has finally invaded one of the last institutions that can still openly require its employees to wear their hair a certain way and unapologetically turns away people who are colorblind. The military can have a standard of dress, fitness and, yes, even height, but they don't have military wives or deployed husbands. They have military spouses.

As a columnist and author, this new lingo has created much confusion for me. When I write, "Military spouses meet once a month for support," how do you know who I'm talking about? Is it deployed service members who meet once a month? Is it the families back home?

And what if I wrote, "Military husbands and wives meet once a month for support"?

You can see how this gets very cumbersome, and how the new, politically correct way of speaking adds quite a bit of word count to a columnist's weekly feature. I long for the days when I could write, "We wives get together monthly for support." Because here's the thing, there aren't any male spouses in my Wives—I mean, Spouse Club!

Editors suggest not using the same word more than once on a single page. For instance, it would be uncreative if I were to use "lingo" a second time in this column. Instead, I'll have to come up with other synonyms. "Jargon," "vernacular" and "terminology" perhaps. Yet I am restricted ("limited," "controlled," "restrained") to the word "spouse" when I'm referring to men and women who are married to someone in the military. I can't even say "dependents," because that's another no-no.

This whole thing, and the fear of it, has become so engrained in my head that the other day I told a telemarketer, "No, my spouse isn't home right now." I immediately laughed because it sounded awkward. But the truth is, "husband" just doesn't roll off my tongue anymore.

When I was growing up as a military BRAT ... I mean, dependent ... oops, I mean, kid? ... my mom was a Navy Wife and took me to Wives Club meetings. The commissary had brown paper bags with "Navy Wife: it's the toughest job in the Navy" printed on them. Being a "Navy Wife" was a big deal, and the Wives Club was like a grown-up secret sorority. I remember sitting on our back porch and watching Mom and the other women pose for pictures that would be sent overseas to their husbands. They blew kisses at the camera, giggled and bonded in a way that only women who are missing their husbands usually can.

I can't help but think those days are gone forever. It's about as politically correct to act like a sorority girl at a Spouse Club meeting as it is to paint Bomber Girls on the side of aircraft. The romance of it is gone. I'm not a Navy Wife. I'm a military spouse. And somehow that feels sterile.

I'm not saying that male spouses aren't important. (And, by "male spouses," of course, I mean men who are married to female service members.) I'm also not saying that men shouldn't be in the Spouse Club or that they personally have in some way taken the romance out of military life. It is not the men or the women who have created this dilemma, but rather it is society's desire to lump us all together and make everyone equal which has. I should be able to call myself a "military wife" without offending anyone else. When my Spouse Club is made up of females, I shouldn't feel ashamed becaues I refer to it as the Wives Club. And when I write that "my husband is a Navy pilot," I shouldn't have to pull out the thesaurus and look for a different word.

Because ultimately, what's happening here is that being a wife isn't the toughest job in the military anymore. But figuring out what to call ourselves is.

It's Like Dating, Only Harder

Making new friends—the process is both a blessing and a curse for military wives. Nevertheless, we are experts at it. We bond quickly with fellow spouses and neighbors over long deployments and harsh conditions, a process I liken to being trapped in an elevator together. I once heard a civilian say that she's never seen anyone except a military wife move in, get involved, make friends, and host supper club ... all before the movers have left her house. Basically, military spouses have this making-friends thing down to a science. So for anyone who's ever struggled with how to meet people in a new city, here are some tips from the pros.

It's Like Dating, Only Harder

Don't let anyone tell you differently. Making new friends is just like dating, only more difficult. When a woman dates a man, she can safely assume that the average male isn't very bright when it comes to social norms and communication. The woman can play tricks with his mind. She can drop hints to help prod the relationship along. The man, more concerned with the miles on his car or his dog's ingrown hair, is none the wiser. Dating a new friend is trickier. Your prospective friend is probably already attuned to subtle clues about your personality. There's no sense in putting on a show. And in the civilian world, there is time for this sort of "dance." Not in the military. There aren't enough months in a military tour to tinker with the customary rules of "courting." We skip right over "how's the weather?" to "I have migraines in the morning, and I once blew a corn kernel out of my nose." In this way, we make friends—real, close friends with a lot of blackmail leverage—fast.
Point: Be your unique self right from the start.

When It's Good It's Good, But When It's Bad ...

Military spouses are lucky to meet many different people throughout the country and world. If you believe in the theory that we learn from every friend, military spouses are pretty darn smart. Like serial daters, we have honed our skills—as far as friendships are concerned—and each successful or failed attempt at making a new friend helps us with the next one. This is one luxury of being a military wife. We move so often, we aren't confronted for the rest of our lives with friendships gone wrong. But if you aren't affiliated with the military, don't despair. You can still build your friend-making techniques. Just practice on a military wife! If it fails, she will move. And yes, there will be another.

Point: Practice really does make perfect. Or, you won't always make a new best friend the first time.

Friends Don't Come to Your Door

Your mother was right: Opportunity won't come knocking, unless you put in a little effort. The same is true with friends. Military spouses know how to work a new neighborhood as soon as they set foot in it. If no one brings house-warming muffins before the boxes are unpacked, it's not uncommon for the newly arrived military wife to take matters into her own hands. I once brought fresh-baked "welcome" cookies to a neighbor who had lived in the neighborhood for five years already. Anything to make a friend. And so, when you look at it this way, it's probably safe to say that opportunity won't come knocking on your door ... but a military spouse might.

Point: Actively seek out friends. Don't wait for them to come to you. (Unless maybe they are a military wife.)

The Address Book

The last and most important thing military spouses know about friendship is this: Duty stations come and go, but friends are forever. Saying goodbye doesn't mean "goodbye." It simply means that your Christmas-card list is about to get much longer.

Point: When you add a new friend to your address book, put their name in ink, but always (always!) write the mailing address in pencil.

You Know You're A Military Wife When ...

They were sitting beside me in the waiting room of a Navy Medical branch clinic. They were talking to each other and smiling, so I knew that they were newly married.

I know what you're thinking: "Sarah, that's so stereotypical, jumping to conclusions and assuming that they are newly married simply because they were talking to each other and smiling. I mean, why didn't you assume something more obvious and reasonable, such as that they were boyfriend and girlfriend?"

Oh, well, that's easy. The young man dressed in a green flight suit couldn't have brought his girlfriend into the clinic. She would not have had an ID card.

So, there I was reading a wrinkled and torn pamphlet about prostate cancer while they held between them the ends of a brochure about their medical benefits. I was alone, and they were huddled so close you'd have thought they were sitting in a teepee. I should also point out that the girl wore a fresh, coordinated outfit that not only looked clean, but it looked ironed, too. I was wearing sneakers with no socks and a red baseball cap, because I don't get dressed up for a Strep-throat culture.

The girl walked to the receptionist's desk to check on her appointment time.

"Last four?" the receptionist said.

The girl looked confused.

"Last four of your husband's social," the woman said.

The girl turned around to her husband, still waiting in the chair, and said, "What's your Social Security number, Honey?"

Right then, there was absolutely no mistaking it. They were newlyweds. You can't be married to someone in the military for too long before you know their Social Security like you know your own shoe size. In fact, I know my husband's "last four" better than I know my own.

All of which got me thinking: just like there is a point at which a woman can no longer hide her pregnancy, there comes a time when a woman is undeniably a military wife. When is that point? It's different for each person. Sometimes it even happens over night, while you are unaware. But eventually we all suffer the same fate: we wake up thinking, when was the last time my mother wrote my address in ink in her address book?

You might also realize you're a military wife when ...

- The sight of US GOVERNMENT on your caller ID no longer freaks you out.
- All your husband's fresh white underwear has his "last four" stamped on the waist band.
- You know the smell of JP-5.
- You know what JP-5 stands for.
- You laugh at "Top Gun." Even harder at Tom Cruise as "Maverick."
- You know that APO isn't a type of dog food.
- Your husband's best friends have names like "GULA," "Wookie," "Rat Boy," and "Dancing Bear."
- Suddenly "GULA," Wookie," "Rat Boy," and "Dancing Bear" seem like affectionate nicknames. (Although, probably not to your civilian mother.)
- You've had five different jobs in four years.
- You've had five different addresses in four years.
- You've had five new best friends in four years.
- Luckily you've had the same husband for five years, but you haven't seen him in three.
- You know that "Haze grey and underway" is not a song by Neil Young.
- When your husband announces he's going to use "the head," you no longer smirk and think, "About time, but I'm still smarter than you."
- You realize that when you're husband is on "cruise," he won't be dining with the captain of the "Love Boat."

- Similarly, you realize that your junior husband won't be dining with any captain.
- You know that your husband will eat in the Mess Hall, and you think that's right where he belongs.
- And last, you definitely know you're a military wife when you're sitting in a waiting room without your husband and you're not the least bit jealous of the girl who doesn't know her husband's "last four." (Even if she was thinner and had better skin.) Because you know, without a doubt, that she's got a lot to learn and a long way to go.

Compartmentalizing: Bad For Moms

One of my favorite things to do when I was little was sit on the garage steps while my dad tinkered with his old '67 Mustang.

"Whatcha doin'?" I'd ask.

"Hmmm?" Dad would answer, his tan corduroy pants sticking out from under the hood.

"Can I help, Dad?"

"Hmmm?"

I would hear the clinking sound of metal tools hitting the cement floor.

"Are you almost done, Dad?"

"Hmmm?"

Then, just to see if he was listening, I'd say, "OK well, I think I'll go get my tongue pierced now."

And he'd say, quite flatly, "Hmmm?"

I'd stomp into the house crying, "Mom, Dad isn't listening to me! I tried talking to him but he just ignores me."

Mom would say, "Tell me, how did he respond when you asked him a question?"

"Well, he went 'Hmmm?'"

"Ah," Mom would say, her face brightening. "Dad's not ignoring you, he's just compartmentalizing again."

Compartmentalizing. Oh, how I hated this word. Dad always said it was just a skill the Navy had taught him. Why then, I wondered, did he utilize this "skill" when he was doing everything else (mowing the lawn, grilling hamburgers, watching NASCAR).

Now I'm grown and married to Dustin, and this compartmentalizing thing has become an issue once again.

ME: "Dustin, are you going to mow the lawn today?"

DUSTIN: "Hmm?"

ME: "I said, 'Are you going to mow the lawn today?' The crab grass is about as tall as our mailbox."

DUSTIN: "Hmm?"

ME: (Just to see if he's listening) "Dustin, quick! Someone's leaving with your golf clubs!"

DUSTIN: "Hmm?"

My friend Dave, who is a source of nearly all things accurate and also happens to be my husband's superior, says this: "I tell every student who checks into the squadron about compartmentalization."

So, there you have it, folks. This "Hmm?" stuff is condoned military behavior.

I looked up "compartmentalize" in the dictionary. Here's what it said: "verb; to separate into compartments."

Hmmm? [Scratching my head]

Deciding that I must finally know the truth behind the military and its compartmentalizing, I went right to the "Horse's Hmm?": "Dad, now that I'm a grown woman, could you please explain compartmentalization to me?"

Turns out, compartmentalizing is a very important skill taught to pilots and others who work in a dangerous setting. The ability to "separate into compartments" allows these men and women to focus on a task without letting their emotions interrupt. For instance, when Dustin is flying, he is able to compartmentalize and forget my nagging about the lawn. When we have fought the night before, he is able to go to work and act as if it never happened, which prevents him from getting distracted.

Indeed, compartmentalizing is important. It's what keeps our loved ones safe. But here's the problem: Often, the ability to compartmentalize transcends to time at home. And I'm convinced it also provides a clever excuse for men to practice the age-old routine of "ignore her and she will eventually go away."

In another strange twist of reality, however, my job as a stay-at-home mom requires a totally different skill: multi-tasking. Multi-tasking is the ability to do all things and to help all people ... at the same time. It means when I'm busy writing a column or folding laundry, I'm also expected to be able to cook dinner, bathe the children, vacuum the living room, and reassure my husband that his hair is not receding. Dave's wife explains it very simply by making juggling motions with her hands and humming a circus tune.

In short, multi-tasking (or, juggling) is the exact opposite of military-approved compartmentalization.

Recently, I decided to drop a few juggling balls and try my hand at focusing on one thing at a time. I got so involved in a project that I lost track of time and got to Ford's school a few minutes late for pick-up. "I thought you'd never come," he said, getting into the car. And then later: "Do you think you could be on time tomorrow, like the other moms."

My brain is decidedly unable to separate into compartments and still function well. And that, my friends, is reason #287 for why I'd never make it in the military, and the only reason I'm mowing the lawn today and Dustin is not.

Public Displays Of Navy Pride Aren't For Everyone

My husband Dustin graduated from the Naval Academy in Annapolis, Md. This is an accomplishment to be proud of, I know, but does it mean I should wear the Academy's mascot (a goat) on everything I own? Am I a lousy Navy wife just because I refuse to wear socks that are blue and gold and 14kt-gold "NA" earrings?

I'd be willing to bet that my mother-in-law has nearly every piece of Naval Academy paraphernalia available. She has goat socks and jewelry, blue and gold blankets and bags, and the mandatory "I'm a Naval Academy Mom" sweatshirt.

Me? First of all, blue has never been a good color on me, and jewelry resembling school mascots is something I purposefully avoid. It's just not my style to wear socks that sing "Anchor's Aweigh" or a rhinestone goat pin on my lapel. I don't wear these things for my own school—why would I wear them for his?

But does this make me an unsupportive wife?

I know I could make Dustin the happiest man alive if I'd just yell "Go Navy!" once after seeing "'97," his class year. But it's not in my nature to be so school-spirited. And if I were to cheer for any class year, it would be '99—my own.

Do goat socks and school chants make a person supportive?

I wish that supporting my husband through flight school and all his various training had been as easy as donning a Naval Academy sweatshirt or a blue and gold barrette in my hair. Unfortunately, helping him has required much more mundane tasks like quizzing him on "EPs" (emergency procedures) and listening patiently as he practiced monotonous briefs. Not very glamorous.

And let's not forget about all the months I've spent alone, taking care of the bills, our children and home while he was at sea.

Can all these acts of sacrifice really be overshadowed by the fact that I don't know the Naval Academy's fight song, or that "Go Navy!" and "Beat Army!" are phrases I have deliberately left out of my vocabulary?

I like to think not.

I agree to put up with weekend duty, moving every three years, and taking out the trash while Dustin is at sea, but I draw the line at displaying any goats on our mantle or decorating the kitchen in blue and gold.

Does this sound selfish? It might to some. For many spouses, school-spirit and "Beat Army!" bumper stickers come naturally and without cost to their own identity. But it wasn't my style to hang a flag with a goat on it from my front door before I married my husband, and I haven't changed since.

Just between you and me, however, I secretly know every verse of the "Navy Hymn," and I can play it from memory on the piano. I walked down the aisle at my wedding carrying a small antique handkerchief that had "USN Wife" embroidered on the corner. And if you look closely at my key chain (the bent handle of a silver spoon from the *USS Lexington*), you will see "USN" engraved ever so lightly on the back.

I might never cheer "'97," but the Navy is entwined deeply into the cloth of who I am. It is the undercurrent of my childhood and adulthood. Yes, I admit that "Anchor's Aweigh" was played at my wedding, and the words "Eternal Father, strong to save" give me goose bumps. But you won't ever see this girl in a "Naval Academy Wife" sweatshirt.

Go Navy!

Military Spouses Deserve Appreciation Every Day

May is National Military Appreciation Month, an umbrella title that encompasses several well-known holidays such as Armed Forces Day and Memorial Day, but also the lesser-known "Military Spouse Appreciation Day," which was May 12th, and well, I missed it. Maybe you did, too.

Military Spouse Appreciation Day isn't quite up to the exposure of Mother's Day, or even Secretaries Day, but it should be. Why are there no Military Spouse Appreciation cards at Hallmark? Why aren't there special "Military Spouse" discounts for Military Spouse Appreciation Day at the department stores?

The answer may be that Military Spouse Day is easy to overlook, and a great majority of people (like me) totally missed it. Is it that military spouses don't demand much attention or praise that this day of honor has slipped under the national radar? Or is that, in the absence of Hallmark cards and flower arrangements designed especially for the occasion, we simply don't know how to commend military spouses?

I think it's probably a mixture of both. So on behalf of military spouses everywhere, here is a short and incomplete list of ways Americans can show their appreciation for military spouses, not just on Military Spouse Day, but all the year through.

Lend a Hand

Military spouses spend a lot of time separated from their service-member loved one and taking care of a house and family. The home repairs alone can feel overwhelming, but add to that the constant shadow of fear and loneliness, and often just getting macaroni-and-cheese on the table is a wearisome task. If you know a military spouse living alone, offer your help occasionally by mowing the grass, taking their car to have its oil changed, or making dinner. Any service member will tell you, just knowing their family back home is being "taken care of" is the greatest support you can give to them as well.

Support the Troops

No matter your political persuasion, use discretion when talking to a military spouse, especially one who's spouse is deployed. There's nothing worse than hearing about "this useless war" when your spouse has no choice in the matter (and neither do you), yet still you are separated for months and months for a cause some people don't believe in. Remember that a military spouse wants to know that his/her spouse's service is not in vain. One great way to show that you are rallying for the spouse and the service member is to fly a flag—on your car, in your yard, from the garage, or even on a sticker or lapel. Outward symbols such as these remind military spouses that although everyone else's life is seemingly "moving on," their loved one's daily sacrifices are not forgotten.

Don't Go MIA

It's a common phenomenon that military spouses come to expect. Once we tell someone, "My husband/wife is in the military," we might as well don a black sheep suit because some people will never look at us the same again. There's something about our situation that makes people uncomfortable. It's the same awkwardness that afflicts people seeing a widow for the first time, I suppose. It's common to hear people say, "Oh, I didn't invite you because I didn't want you to feel like a fifth wheel...with your husband gone and all," or, "We didn't think you'd want to join our supper club because you'll be moving in a few years, won't you?" Military spouses—especially military spouses!—need connections and friendships just like anyone else. Don't abandon your military-spouse friend because you don't know what to say or you're afraid she'll eventually move. Take time to get to know military spouses. They are some of the most fascinating people in the world.

Each and every day remember that there are thousands of men and women who sacrifice for our country without even leaving the house. They are watching children, maintaining a home, and supporting a service member—all without asking for much in return—and that deserves our greatest admiration. Hallmark card, or no Hallmark card.

The Military

Military Marriage:

It Should Come With A Warning.

Don't Say I Didn't Warn You

My husband Dustin didn't come with instructions (except for my mother-in-law's insistence that he be fed often), nor did he come with a warning, but I think life would be easier if he had.

So if I could rewrite his marriage proposal to me, making it more fair and forewarning, this is what I would have had him say:

"My dear Sarah—dear, sweet, perfect, wonderful Sarah—would you do the honor of being my wife and sharing your life with me?

But wait, before you answer, let me tell you a little about the job.

First of all, I am a Navy pilot, and I move often. We will have very little control over when or where we go, and sometimes we will be told we are moving one place, only to find out at the last minute we are going somewhere else. Are you good with flexibility? Can you pack and unpack quickly?

There will be times that you have to handle our moves by yourself because I go out to sea for six months at a time. Now, judging by your expression, I won't go into detail now about the additional months I'll spend on detachments and assignments, because, Sarah, I really want you to say 'yes' today.

Are you a sentimental person at all? I'll probably miss a lot of Christmases, birthdays and anniversaries. But we can always celebrate when I get back, and I'll be sure to call you from the boat on Valentine's Day. (Keep in mind, however, that calls from the ship are expensive, so we'll have to keep it short.) Oh, and don't count on me being there when you have our babies either.

How good are you with home repairs and handling crises? Since I will be gone 60 percent of our life, you will be responsible for fixing toilets, fertilizing the lawn, and dealing with hurricanes, tornadoes, and any other natural disaster that comes your way.

You will also be responsible for coming up with new and inventive ways to remove the smell of JP5 (jet fuel) from the clothes I bring home from the boat, and you will spend a lot of time washing and drying flight suits.

How quick are you with the iron, and can you hem pants? There will be times I forget to tell you that I need my uniform for certain events, and at the last minute I will depend on you to pick it up from the cleaners. Are you good at finding lost covers (military hats), belts, and uniform T-shirts?

Oh, and are you attached to your career plans at all? It may be hard for you to build a career as we move from place to place. And are you a worrier? My job is dangerous, and when I'm on deployment you might not hear from me for long stretches at a time. Sometimes I may not be able to tell you where I am at all. You will need to handle these situations with grace and dignity and try to go on with your normal life without crying every time you see someone else's husband coming home for dinner.

Try not to dwell on the magnitude of my job or the commitment I have made to the country. I am at the mercy of my command, and though I will treasure you and our family above all things, at times it will seem like I am married to the Navy and that I spend more time on the boat than I do at home.

But you will get used to the feeling of being alone. Trust me.

Lastly let me say this: Through our time and travels with the Navy, you will meet some of the best friends of your life, and you will see and do things you never thought possible. You will join the ranks of all other military spouses who are some of the strongest women in the world, and you will have the personal satisfaction that as my wife you have made enormous sacrifices (with little reward or commendation, although I will try to send flowers occasionally), but you have helped me to serve our country and protect its freedom. For that, I (and others) will always be grateful.

So if all of this sounds good to you, I'll need your answer soon. I have to report to duty in ten minutes. Oh, and can you plan a quick wedding? We'll be moving next month.

And Sarah, don't say I didn't warn you."

You Can't Take The Military Out Of The Man

What's worse than taking down Christmas decorations after the holidays? Apparently, according to Dustin, it is taking them down ... while your father-in-law watches.

But before I get to that, first I should tell you that we spent the holidays with my whole family—my two brothers and their wives, my brother's mother-in-law, my parents, and my grandmother—at a resort in Florida. It was the perfect setting because no one was responsible for cleaning dishes and washing dirty towels. No, it wasn't because the resort did it for us. Mom did. My mom is the planner. She can put together an itinerary for fun (while supervising my children) quicker than the rest of us can get out of bed at 10 o'clock in the morning. In fact, by the time my day finally had started at a quarter past noon, I was already three items behind on Mom's list.

"But I don't want to be the planner," Mom said with a pen in one hand and notepaper in the other. "All of you *make* me the planner."

This is mostly true. We kids (and by that I mean Dustin, me, my brothers and their wives) spent our vacation sitting around playing 20Q, a handheld, computerized version of the traditional "20 Questions" game, which can read your mind—just like a mother, come to think of it. Santa brought the toy for my five-year-old son Ford, with no clue whatsoever how much fun the "adults" would have with it instead. Honest, Santa didn't know.

So while we, ahem, adults wracked our brains to find the oddest, most obscure word (something like "poop") for 20Q to guess, Mom busied herself making sure everyone was fed and wearing clean clothes. Meanwhile, in between rounds of 20Q, my older brother, Will, taught Ford how to burp super loud and blame it on someone else. My other brother, Van, showed Owen, 3, how to get his new toy fire truck to make really obnoxious noises. My dad, or "Pop" as everyone except Dustin calls him, just sat in the corner smiling. And really, this is what family gatherings are all about, aren't they? It's all fun and games until someone ends up with stitches—which, by the way, happened on the last day of our trip when Doris ran her leg into the staircase.

So why doesn't Dustin call my dad Pop? Well, my dad is retired Navy, and for a brief period of time, he and Dustin were on the same ship together. Technically, my boy-scout of a husband only sees my dad as his superior, which makes family gatherings even more interesting. There's nothing like hearing someone say, "Please pass the potatoes Mr. Rutherford, Sir," over Thanksgiving dinner.

This is also why Dustin blushed sheepishly and tried not to laugh (although I know he wanted to) when 20Q guessed "poop" correctly.

You can take the man out of the military, but you can't take the military out of the man. Or, something like that.

So anyway, after four days at the resort, we returned home with just my parents and Doris, and immediately upon entering the house, my mom said, "Who's ready to take down these Christmas decorations and optimize your storage space?" I pretended not to hear her, but Dustin, the kind man that he is, fell prey to Mom's Martha-Stewart moment and wound up wrapping Christmas ornaments and labeling boxes while my dad and I tried to get 20Q to guess "spontaneous combustion."

Next thing I knew, Dustin was dragging our seven-foot Christmas tree—still in its base, and dripping water—through the living room. His face was flushed and tense, like someone coming off the battlefield—my mom's organizing battle field. Then, in what I guess was a harried attempt to just get it over with, but ended up being a Clark-Griswald moment instead, Dustin shoved the behemoth tree through the front door top first so that the stand caught on the wall, pine needles fell like rain, and large branches made the worst scratching sound ever against the paint on our front door.

When that didn't work, Dustin stood back, scratched his head ... and tried the same maneuver again.

Pop looked up from our game and smiled. "Important safety tip, Dustin," he said. "Always take the tree bottom first through the door."

Then Dad and I looked at each other, and I said, "Oh, behemoth! Let's see if 20Q can guess behemoth."

Right then and there, it was pretty much decided—in Dustin's mind, at least—that Pop will always be "Sir" to him.

Military Men, Life Are Ironic

Military life is full of ironies. As the wife of an active-duty service member, for instance, I am classified as a "dependent," a term that implies weakness, when in fact, I have to be extremely self-reliant while my husband is deployed.

Military families are also accustomed to spontaneity, as in, "Honey, we're moving across country next month," and, "I'm leaving for Iraq on Monday." And yet, military life in general offers many constants: job security and healthcare, to name just two. We may not know where or when we'll be moving, but we know our spouse will have a job and we will have healthcare when we get there.

Also, military service members are the most affected by the government's decisions to go to war, but they are some of the last to speak out about it. Military men and women have built their careers around defending our country, but they are the ones who don't necessarily want to put their skills (going to war) to use. In how many other careers do you train for something that you hope will never happen?

The greatest irony of all, however, may be that military men are typically loaded with testosterone and have a desire to rescue and save others, but they attract mates who initially might seem needy and loaded with estrogen. Except that over time, these women prove to be stronger than their husbands in many ways. And then, irony of all ironies, the very system that helped spur these women into independence sometimes comes back to punish them for it.

I can't tell you how many times people ask my husband, "Why do you let your wife write that stuff in the newspaper?" Or, "I'd never let my wife do that." Interesting when you consider that my position as a military wife largely influenced my tendency to be outspoken and independent. The same people who question my husband for "allowing" his wife to be so visible and opinionated would probably also criticize him if I was weak while he was away (which, for the record, I basically was when we were first married, and yes, I was criticized for it).

All of which has sometimes led me to believe that it is the military men who are conflicted about what they want. In the beginning, they are the rescuer, the "man in uniform." Then they leave for six months and naturally want their spouse to rise to the occasion. Upon return, many military men want their wife to revert back to the typical wifely role, and it has been my experience that more than a few wives are loathe to do so. This, by the way, leads to the mostly inevitable fights that plague homecomings.

At my husband's first squadron, I was not popular with some of his co-workers. I'm told the animosity stemmed from my tendency to be more dominate than my husband. I am the extrovert; he is the introvert. How dare a military wife be more outspoken than her husband?

I'm also told that the co-workers' feelings came from one instance when I asked my husband not to attend a no-wives-allowed party. Silly me, I didn't realize how selfish it was to request such a thing the night after our son had been in the hospital with a concussion. Shame on me for putting my family first, a skill I've honed through months of surviving deployments and sudden moves.

Since that experience, I've observed many military gatherings and have noticed that usually the most confident, outspoken "Dependent" is the least liked by her husband's peers. Some women are just better at hiding their feisty side, I suppose, and some of us can't seem to keep it under wraps.

Luckily, my husband is proud to be married to the latter. "Sarah makes me more interesting," he's been known to say. He appreciates the way I've grown and changed.

It's a good thing. To squash my independence or stifle my confidence, and then turn around and expect me to pack up our house on short-notice and raise three children alone would be, well, highly ironic.

Taming The Military In-Laws

Leading up to a ship's homecoming, military Spouse Clubs are abuzz with the following reunion topics: (1) what to wear, (2) what not to wear, and (3) how to keep the in-laws at bay.

I forgot about this ritual until recently, when I spoke to a group of new military wives whose husbands are about to embark on their first deployment. Going into the meeting, I thought I was prepared for what the wives would want to know. I was ready to tell them about staying busy and using a support network. But after I finished what I thought was an important spiel, the hands went up, eager with questions, and the women wanted to know (1) what to wear, (2) what not to wear, (3) and how to keep the in-laws away.

What to wear is a matter of personal preference, and I never wish to open that can of what I'll call "angry fan mail." But I am willing to take a risk with the last question, because after I was done speaking that night, one of the women said, "Could you write a column about the in-law thing so we can forward it to our families as a little hint-hint?"

What an interesting concept, I thought. And how clever! There are instruction books for military spouses and service members, but who's telling the in-laws how to behave?

So, here are a few guidelines to tame your in-laws and keep the peace at home. Feel free to forward this to troublemakers if you'd like, but only at your own risk. Emotions run high pre-homecoming, but remember: when it's all said and done, these are still your in-laws, the people who will be present at a majority of your family's holidays and birthdays.

In-Laws Should Not be at the Homecoming

There, I've said it. And I know you're itching to say it, too. When it comes to homecoming, you and your spouse alone deserve the romance and excitement surrounding it. If your family has trouble understanding, gently say, "Mom, remember how you didn't want to go on our honeymoon with us? And remember how I didn't take you to the Senior Prom?" If necessary, refer to homecoming as "Our Second Honeymoon."

Be Sensitive Reporting Contact

There's not much worse than this when it comes to in-laws: you've been waiting for your husband to call from a foreign port. You sit by the phone anxious and excited. And when it finally rings, it is your mother-in-law saying, "Guess who just called me? It was so great to hear his voice!"

Communicating from the ship is difficult. It's common for emails to arrive out of sync and for phone lines to drop mid-call. To avoid hurt feelings, in-laws should be sensitive when boasting to the wife about their own phone calls and/or emails.

Don't Embarrass Your Child

Some mothers treat grown-up sons like little boys. To each his own, but here's a word of caution: Your son will be humiliated by his peers if you send him a care package with underwear, teddy bears (and any other stuffed animal, for that matter), or framed childhood pictures of him taking a bath. No, it doesn't matter that "the wife" sent him a talking Winnie the Pooh. What's considered acceptable for her does not apply to anyone else.

Stay Visible

I hear stories about in-laws suddenly becoming incognito during a deployment. I guess the theory is, "My son's not at home, so why should I call his house?" Some daughters-in-law feel nearly invisible to their spouse's parents while he is away. But here's a little secret: The wife gets all the info from the squadron/unit. Tell your in-laws this, and I guarantee the phones will ring. Of course, if you'd rather they didn't call, well, that's another column.

In closing, my guess is that these guidelines for a harmonious in-law relationship will ruffle some feathers ... and I'm going to hear about it. But let me save you some trouble and give you the name of a person to contact if you'd like to send "angry fan mail." Her name is, Dustin's Mom. That's right, my mother-in-law. Because here's the funny thing, as a former military wife herself, she agrees with me!

.

Homecoming: Some Mothers Just Don't Understand

Several weeks ago, I wrote a column about in-laws, and specifically, how they shouldn't be present at military homecomings. My comments ruffled more than a few mothers-in-law's feathers, but surprisingly few wives'. Most shocking of all, however, was the fact that no one took my advice to send their comments straight to my own mother-in-law instead of to me.

The next morning after that column appeared, I was slammed with angry messages from mothers, and supportive ones from their daughters-in-law (imagine that!). An online forum was flooded with reactions to the piece, and a battle of messages was fought between mothers and wives for several weeks.

Apparently, I've touched a nerve.

Here is a sampling of what some readers had to say:

"Sorry, but shame on you. You had an opportunity to unite people who were hurting rather than to be divisive."

"Some families actually love each other ... their love is something they have in common and share, rather than selfishly [keep] only for themselves."

"Right on! I am the mother of two military sons and a military daughter-in-law, and have never been present at their return from deployments."

"I just wanted to say thanks ... I laughed till I cried and then forwarded it to my soldier."

"Sorry, but I disagree with your viewpoint, and family values ... [homecoming] is the reward for the nights you cried your eyes out and prayed till you had no more words ... I just think we need to be more inclusive, and not so insecure."

After reading the replies, I've come to this one realization: mothers-in-law are crazy!

No, I'm only kidding.

What I meant to say is that mothers and wives have a serious case of misunderstanding each other.

When a man leaves for deployment, it is an entirely different experience for his wife than it is for his mother. Chances are, the mother is already accustomed to not seeing her son on a regular basis. And hopefully, he isn't her main source of support. But for the wife, the husband's absence is not only a life-altering experience, it is a day-to-day altering one as well.

This is why homecoming is so important to the wife. She has not only worried and prayed as much as the mother has, but she has also been both mother and father to her children, taken care of a house, eaten hundreds of meals alone, and gone to bed night after night without her spouse.

I liken the experience of homecoming to having your first baby. I didn't invite my mother-in-law into the delivery room, but that wasn't because I was being selfish. Ford's birth affected Dustin and me in a different way than it did her, and I didn't feel obligated to share the experience with anyone else. (That, plus a few hundred other reasons involving modesty and hospital gowns, of course.)

However, if my Inbox is any indication, there are several sides to this story, and I admit I don't fully understand the mothers'. Yet someday, maybe I will. I have two sons, and eventually I will be "one of them," the dreaded "mother-in-law." I'm sure I'll make my share of mistakes that irritate my daughters-in-law, and I'll probably even earn myself a few new nicknames, too.

But if Ford and Owen join the military, I can promise you this: I won't be at homecoming.

(And, oh, I won't be in the delivery room either.)

The Column That Will Not Die

A few years ago, I wrote a column suggesting that mothers-in-law should not attend a service member's homecoming if their son or daughter is married, and especially if they have specifically requested to have time alone first.

Initially I referred to the column as "the mother-in-law one" because the very next morning after it was published, I received dozens of scathing messages from angry mothers. For the record, dozens more service members and their spouses were plenty happy with my column and even were relieved to know that when they are dealing with insulted in-laws and parents, they can say, "Well, Sarah Smiley said it first!"

Lately though, I call the infamous column "the one that will not die," because it seems to resurface when I'm busy writing a column that will bother someone else (such as the military hospital or the commissary). The mother-in-law column has probably traveled the globe via forwarded emails, spurned alternately by validated wives and incensed mothers. And every now and then, someone sends me a message of approval or contempt. When I do interviews, more often than not, the reporter eventually asks, with a playful smile on their face, "So what about that mother-in-law issue?"

Apparently I had dared to go where most happily married women do not—I had tread on the mother-in-law. And if you think a scorned lover can get wound up tighter than a jack-in-the-box, you haven't messed with a mother.

Yet, the supportive emails assure me that this problem of mothers-in-law at homecoming is not only universally weighed and measured, it has been a bone of contention since the military has been coming home in the first place. It amazes me how timely it remains.

So first, let's review the issue as a whole and why otherwise wonderful and pleasant mothers-in-law have become so problematic for some couples near homecoming. For many husbands and wives, military homecomings are like a honeymoon. Some people have even claimed that homecoming is more intimate and exciting than their wedding. But besides the celebration, homecoming can also be a very intense and emotional time, as husband and wife reconnect after months spent apart. It takes time to reunite as a family, and this process can sometimes be hindered by guests.

"So why can't a mother-in-law just come to the actual homecoming and then go home and leave the couple alone?" you ask.

Because most military families don't live near their in-laws. For a mother-in-law to be at homecoming, she usually has to make a special trip, which makes the couple feel obligated to host and entertain her at a time when their focus should be on each other.

A great many mothers understand this predicament and wait a few days, or even weeks, before making the trip to see their loved ones. But if you have a unenlightened mother on your hands and you're wondering how to deal with her, here's a quick guide to the two most common types of prickly mothers-in-law.

The Mother of All Mothers

This mother might as well be Mother Nature because she was apparently born to mother everyone, including you, but especially her beloved son. You will never clean, cook or raise children good enough to suit her. She can always do it better. And by the way, you're lousy at taking care of her son. As homecoming approaches, this mother might be worried about her son's first dinner at home and whether or not he'll have clean sheets on the bed. To keep her at bay, assure her that you've sufficiently planned for your husband's arrival. Then make reservations at your husband's favorite restaurant and be done with it. She never has to know.

The Possessive Mother

You took her son away, and now she will never forgive you. In her mind, this mother truly believes that your husband would rather spend his first night home eating lasagna with his mother than ... well, you know ... with his wife. The Possessive Mother needs to be at homecoming because, unfortunately, yours is a marriage of three, not two. She is the "other woman." The only way to satisfy this mother-in-law is to die or get a divorce, and I strongly discourage both.

Talk to your husband and come up with a plan together. Talk about your expectations for homecoming ahead of time so that you're both on the same page. And if your mother-in-law gets mad because she's not invited, don't celebrate yet. You might think this means she'll never bother you again. Unfortunately, it only means she'll hate you even more than she already does. She will always love her son. You never can win, so you might as well have the homecoming of your dreams.

Excuse Me,
I'm Trying To Have A Baby

"I did a WESTPAC back then," the man said. "I flew with those helo guys. They're great. Do you know [so-and-so]?"

Dustin moved into proper sea-story posture (hands out in front, ready to simulate aircraft, just in case), and said, "Yeah, those guys went through flight school with me. I haven't talked to them in years."

Just another typical exchange between two military guys. Given more time, they would have segued into stories about landing on carriers, something similar to fishermen comparing the size of their catch. I rolled my eyes, and though I knew a good military wife should feign interest, I couldn't. You see, I was in labor, and it was my husband and the doctor swapping stories over the foot of my labor and delivery bed. Yes, of all the things Dustin has done—taking the boys to the wrong Chik-fil-A for their birthday party, for example—this will rank right up there as one of the most memorable.

When the doctor left the room, Dustin turned to me and said, "Isn't it cool that he was on that cruise?"

Now remember, I was in active labor, anxiously awaiting my epidural. Hopefully you understand why I snapped and said, "Not when I'm trying to have a baby, dammit."

Dustin, realizing his mistake, quickly said, "OK, it's all about you now."

I can only imagine that it's hard for a military man like my husband, in a military hospital with his pregnant wife, to keep the two separate. When the doctor came back in to deliver our baby, he never mentioned that WESTPAC again. Neither did Dustin. No one, not even pilots bursting at the seams with sea stories, messes with a woman about to have a baby.

But, alas, this is where the jokes end.

I couldn't wait to write and tell you about the birth of our third son, Lindell Grant Smiley, on January 9th. I knew the experience would provide plenty of good writing material. In fact, during the above scenario, despite my pain and anxiety, I remember thinking, "Oh, this will be a column."

Yet now, as I sit here plucking away at the keyboard, I have no more snarky comments, no complaints, no it-would-be-funny-if-it-weren't-so-true stories. Instead, I am filled with gratitude and appreciation for the care I received at the military hospital.

Wow, did I just write that?

I've made my share of jokes about long lines at the pharmacy and the condition of some military hospitals. But two weeks ago, when the Navy hospital became my temporary home for the birth of our son, I was reminded of something very important. Mainly, it isn't the buildings or waiting-room comforts that shape our experiences. It is the people. When you have good people, the ceiling could fall apart into pieces to the floor (which it did when I was getting lab work done one day), and still you walk away feeling grateful.

Two weeks ago, I had good people. I had the nurse who held my hand and smoothed my hair; the off-duty doctor who came in the middle of the night to deliver my baby, just because he promised he would; and the pediatrician who patiently and personally offered reassurance when our baby was sick. And this is just to name a few.

My experience reminds me of a trip to the hospital vending machine. (Bear with me here.) First, the vending machine ate my dollar and offered no caffeine in return. I stared at the glowing red light and cried. Then I shuffled back to my room, searched for more change, and returned to the lobby for a second try. On the way, I caught myself thinking, "This is so typical. I should have known that THIS machine in THIS hospital would be broken." I deposited my change anyway, hopelessly pressed a button, and BAM, not one, not two, but *four* diet sodas fell out of the machine. Jackpot.

As I walked back to my room with the cold, wet load of sodas in my arm, it occurred to me that I often approach military-life situations in the same way. At first I am skeptical and pessimistic. But once you get past the endless sea stories, tiresome clichés, and broken machines, you find a priceless treasure, which is, namely, the military's people.

Christmas Cards Create Time Warp

This time of year is a time warp for most of us. We venture into the attic to get Christmas lights and ornaments, where we are sidetracked by a box full of our son's outgrown infant clothes. We stop to think about how much he has grown, then somehow, eventually, we are sitting on the unfinished, splintery plywood floor looking at our high school yearbook and wondering what ever happened to that girl we sat next to on the bus in ninth grade.

Yet if this time of year is a time warp for the general population, it is a virtual time-traveling machine for military families. Our pre-holiday experience differs from that of most other people in specific ways. First, as military families, we are more likely to know where the Christmas lights are located, having just put them in the attic after our most recent move two years ago, and thanks to the movers' note on the box that reads: Hollyday Lites.

Likewise, when we settle onto the attic floor, ready for a trip down Memory Lane with scrapbooks, baby clothes, and everything else not related to the task at hand (finding the Christmas lights, remember?), there is a good chance that we just did this same thing after the aforementioned move, and probably during the holiday in between, too. While civilians might only see the contents of their attics when they are in search of holiday decorations, military families have packed and moved their attics more times than they can count on one hand.

Sorting through Christmas ornaments in particular is a real heady experience for military families. It's not uncommon to find military wives unwrapping Christmas ornaments and saying with alternating fondness and disdain, "Oh, this is from the year we lived in California. This one is from the cross-country move of 2000. And this one—*this one*—well, it's from the nine months we lived in San Diego."

But perhaps the most quintessential military holiday experience is that of sitting down to do the year's Christmas cards. Two weeks ago, I opened my address book to begin this process. Already, by the time I got to the first section marked "A" for last names beginning with that letter, I felt defeated.

"Dustin, do the Adams still live in Rhode Island or have they transferred?" I called out to my husband in the other room.

"Last I heard they were in Washington," he yelled back.

"Well, the address I have here is for Texas, so it must be a really old one."

I addressed the envelope using the latest and best information I had, knowing with great certainty that the card would end up returned to me as "undeliverable." For every 10 Christmas cards military families send out, approximately one bounces back. This creates frustration, but also unique opportunities to reconnect with lost friends. When I got to the "Js," for example, I asked Dustin, "So where are the Joneses now? Have they moved yet? Do they still live in this country? Or are they overseas?" My address book had four entries for the Jones family; all of them were crossed out. You fill up a lot of address-book pages when you and your friends move every three years.

"I need to call them," Dustin yelled back, speaking of the Joneses. "I haven't talked to him in a long time."

Suddenly, despite still being in separate rooms, Dustin and I were calling out funny memories and stories about the Joneses.

When I got to the "P's," the telephone rang and I didn't recognize the number on the caller ID. "Who do we know that's still in Annapolis?" I yelled to Dustin. Next thing I knew, Dustin was on the phone shouting, "Dave, Melvin! What's up guys?"

Oh, how funny, I thought. Even they (meaning Dave and Melvin) got caught up in the time machine of the holidays. Dave and Melvin must have been doing Christmas cards with their wives, I reasoned, when they came across Dustin's name and decided they hadn't talked to him in a long time.

But I really should have known, because after all, we're talking about men here. And, specifically, we're talking about military men.

While I was smiling to myself thinking about these guys getting all sentimental about the holidays and relocating lost pals, the real reason Melvin and Dave had called my husband was to talk about the Army/Navy football game.

Some things never change, no matter what stage of the time warp you are in.

Always Pin His Wings On

Dustin got his naval aviator wings September 1999, in Pensacola, Fla. The date really isn't relevant (although I'm sure it's very relevant to the military), except that it was only eight weeks after our wedding. This is when Dustin and I were both young, thin and without children. We went to the after-party and didn't worry about a babysitter. I wore shorts and didn't think about my legs. Dustin had more hair, less forehead.

But mostly, what our youth and new marriage meant was that I still felt like my husband was on loan from his parents. Dustin called his parents' house, not our apartment, "home." We felt at the mercy of our parents and their plans for family holidays. My in-laws knew more about Dustin than I did. (Keep all this in mind when I tell you about the winging ceremony.)

Somewhere along the way, while planning for the upcoming winging and deluge of relatives, an unforeseen quandary was brought to my attention: Who would pin on Dustin's wings, his dad (a former Navy pilot) or me?

"Your dad will, of course," I said to Dustin. I still felt like he belonged to them, not me.

"But I want you to do it," Dustin said. He was excited about being married and desired to stay that way.

Then Dustin's dad mentioned that he'd like to give Dustin his old aviator wings, and that pretty much sealed the deal. How could I pin my father-in-law's heirloom wings on my husband?

Dustin, still feeling uneasy about the situation and perhaps realizing that eventually the whole thing would explode in his face (he's such a smart man), came up with a deal. His dad would do the ceremonial pinning, but then Dustin would present me with an aviator sweetheart pin.

The Military

This sounded good to me. Everyone was happy.

As the ceremony drew near, however, I began to feel upset. I thought, "Why should my father-in-law do the wings when I'm the one who's kept dinner warm when Dustin's flights went late? Aren't I the one who unpacked our apartment in one day, only to pack it all up again seven weeks later? Didn't I help Dustin practice his emergency procedures? Wasn't I the one who put my career on hold, waiting to get settled at the next duty station?" So my father-in-law gave Dustin life. I realize that ... but still!

Dustin searched for the best sweetheart pin to show how much he appreciated all I had done for him. "And it will be you and me—a team—when I give you this at the ceremony," he told me.

If you've never been to a winging, it's like a graduation, except everyone is in uniform, no one jumps off the stage and does the peace sign for their classmates, and the "graduates" aren't headed to careers of their own choosing. They're going where Uncle Sam sends them (and some of their wives aren't happy about it).

When my husband was called on stage, my in-laws and I followed, just like every other family. Unlike every other group, however, my father-in-law gave a speech before pinning on Dustin's wings. (This is the first reason why everyone from that winging class usually remembers the Smileys.) Once my father-in-law finished and Dustin was "winged," Dustin turned to me, presumably to give me my pin. He hugged me and whispered in my ear. I thought he whispered, "I love you." So I said quite loudly, "I love you, too!" Then he whispered again, "No, I forgot it. I forgot the pin. I don't have it."

A second later we were all shuffled off stage. I was crying. (This is the second reason why everyone from that winging class usually remembers the Smileys.)

I hate to make this about me, but well, as any military wife knows, our husband's career asks a lot of us. It's a team effort. Wingings and promotions are often meant to recognize the force behind the man/woman as much as they are to recognize the active-duty service member.

"At my first promotion," Dustin promised later, "it will be you who does the honors."

That moment came last week.

I had almost forgotten about Dustin's upcoming promotion to Lieutenant Commander, and maybe that was on purpose. It's not that

I'm not proud of my husband or glad to be in a new pay grade, but, well, "Lieutenant Commander" sounds so old. Dustin becoming "Lt. Cmdr. Smiley" the same year that I turned 30—the same year I discovered that I have high blood pressure and was prescribed my first pair of glasses—confirms one thing: We aren't the hip, young couple we used to be. (Some might argue that we never were hip, but whatever.)

"Lt. Smiley" had such a ring to it—a "Top-Gun" Maverick kind of feel. Being married to a Lieutenant is like being married to someone in a fraternity, only the Lieutenants make better money and don't go home to their parents at Christmas. It's the best of both worlds. And if Lieutenants are the "frat guys" of the Navy, then Lieutenant Commanders are kind of like the professors. They are too old to participate in most of the fun, yet still too young to give it up entirely.

When Dustin was at his first squadron, I remember planning parties and debating as to whether or not we should invite the "O-4's," (a nickname for Lieutenant Commanders, derived from the title of their pay grade). It wasn't that we didn't like the Lieutenant Commanders, or that we were trying to be exclusive, but the young guys could relax if the O-4's weren't there.

And now Dustin is an O-4.

I suspect that we are being crossed off party lists as I write this.

So anyway, I might have purposefully forgotten that Dustin was moving beyond his Lieutenant days, until June 1. We had just picked up my 87-year-old grandmother, Doris, for my annual three-week vacation with her. Dustin was driving me, Doris, and the kids from Florida to Virginia, then flying home, where he would be working very hard (that's for his Commanding Officer), while we continued to play. The car ride would take two days. We had just left a hotel somewhere in Georgia when a few miles down the road, Dustin said, "Oh, by the way, I'm a Lieutenant Commander today." I felt an age spot appear under my left eye just as he said it.

Doris, sitting in the backseat, said, "What does that mean exactly, Dustin?"

"It means you have to call me 'Sir' now," Dustin said.

Dustin's humor is often dry, and sometimes misunderstood, as it was then. Doris folded her arms across her chest and huffed a highly indignant, "Well!"

Doris has always said that Dustin is "Number Two." My dad,

Doris's son-in-law, is her "Number One." It is Doris's own personal rank structure for the in-lawed men in her life. When Dustin made his little joke about Doris calling him "Sir," I sensed that he had swiftly moved down the ranks to become "Number Five."

Dustin's actual promotion ceremony, however, wouldn't be until one month later, when the kids and I returned from our vacation. Early one Monday morning, we filed into Dustin's squadron's Ready Room and watched as the Commanding Officer (CO) led Dustin in a reaffirmation of his oath. It felt like Dustin's winging all over again, only my father-in-law wasn't there giving a speech and I wasn't expecting a sweetheart pin. My expectations were decidedly low this time. I just wanted the kids to behave and for my hips to look slim in the pictures. When the CO asked who would pin the new oak leafs on Dustin's uniform, I didn't hesitate. Of course I would do it.

In the beginning of our marriage, at Dustin's winging, I had wondered if it was my place to pin his wings on. Two weeks ago, at Dustin's promotion, there was no question. We have been married eight years. Dustin has been gone for deployments and various other military duties a good percentage of that time. I have been manning the homefront. It's a team effort. Dustin's promotion felt like an achievement for both of us, a reminder of how far we've come and how invested we are in this military lifestyle.

But that still doesn't mean that we're on the invite list for any more Lieutenant parties. Which is OK, really, because we probably couldn't find a babysitter anyway, and Dustin tends to fall asleep watching the evening news.

Relocating:
Greet The Moving Van With Donuts.

Q&A About Military Moves

My husband just received orders across country, and we are expected to be there in three months. I don't think our house will sell before then. Will the military sell it for us?

It's true that many companies have a buy-out program, which basically means that if your company asks you to move, they will buy your house and sell it for you.

The military is not one of these organizations.

"But how does the military expect me to sell my house?" you ask. "Especially in this market. How can they ask us to move and then not help us with the house?"

The military never said that you had to live in a home. That's what base housing is for. They also never said you had to own anything. In fact, if the military had its way, not only would your husband not have a house, he wouldn't be married either. Then Uncle Sam could put him up in the Bachelor Officer's/Enlisted Quarters (BO/EQ) for like $11.00 a day.

Things like spouses, families, school years, mortgages and real estate are all inconveniences that the military would rather have your husband deal with on his own time that he doesn't have. No wait. I take that back. The military wants you—the spouse—to deal with these things. Your husband doesn't know what to do or where to go unless the military has ordered it. This leaves you as the person responsible for making sure that the house sells and everything from the children to the computer end up in the same location that Uncle Sam has sent your spouse.

But the military will move our things for us, right? That's good news, isn't it?

Yes, the military will send a van and four men that you don't know to pack up all your belongings and put them on a truck headed to what you hope is the same destination as you and your family. You will find, however, that because you are military and not the actual person paying the bill, these four men you don't know won't really care if they pack your husband's grass-stained work shoes with your grandmother's white linen table cloth.

The secret handshake, if you will, for getting excellent service from the four men that you don't know is making donuts available to them in the morning and then pretending not to notice when they take a two-hour lunch break on your back porch.

Donuts. Got it. That sounds easy enough. So moving day will be fairly hassle-free then?

No. Moving day will still be hell. In the same way that going to Disney World always seems like a good idea until you are walking through the gates, you will think that you have everything organized and ready for an efficient move. And then you will quickly learn otherwise.

You see, often we forget that moving means packing up all of our belongings — plates, napkins, skillets....beds — until about 4 o'clock in the afternoon on the first day of the move, when suddenly we realize that it sure would be nice to have something other than a box to sit on. Likewise, "camping out" on the living room floor always seems super fun. Until you are doing it.

You can always hope that a nice neighbor or friend will invite you over to dinner that first night, when your house is almost completely dismantled. But use caution here as well. After eight hours of being in a house where things (sofas, cabinets, cushions) that have been in the same place for years are suddenly moved, kicking up a surprising amount of dirt, dust and stale Cheerioes, you won't smell so great. The very best friends will offer you dinner and their shower.

What happens when we get to our destination? Does the military unpack for us?

You are assuming that your belongings, like luggage at the airport, will get to your destination. But, just in case it does; no, the military will not unpack for you. Four new men that you don't know, who have been hired by the military, may or may not unpack for you. But why not just do this the way every other military family does? Open and unpack the necessary boxes, then shove all the rest in your new attic. Don't even take the tape off these boxes. Some people have gone through their whole military careers with boxes that they have not opened in ten moves. Then one day, when they finally retire, they open the boxes, now tagged with moving stickers in every sort of color, only to find that the boxes are filled with their trash.

The movers will pack my trash can without emptying it first? Yes.

Finding A Home The Military Way

Surprisingly, military families know a great deal about owning a home. I say surprisingly because one would think that military families that move every few years would be the last to know anything about owning a home. Renting a house or "How to Make Base Housing Livable," maybe, but owning a home?

Yes.

In fact, some military families own quite a few homes scattered across the country that they'd love to get rid of, if, say, you happen to be in the market. Because if there is one thing military families know about more than owning a home, it's selling a home.

You might be wondering, why do military families bother to buy a house if they're just going to move again so soon?

We buy homes for the same reasons that anyone else does. Namely, to spend our Saturday morning at Home Depot in search of shoe moulding to match our floor that has a stain the size of Oregon on it, and we don't want to think about how it might have gotten there or why we never saw it before we bought the house, so we put a chair over the top of it and decide to worry instead about the shoe moulding—why it pops up on the left side, and where the Barbie-sized nail that once held it in place might have gone and whether or not the dog buried it.

I mean really, what would life be without going on a weekly trip to the garden shop with a batch of suspicious weeds in our hands and leaving with a can of toxins that will destroy everything we just planted last weekend but somehow inspire the dandelions to grow even faster? Military families don't want to miss out on these joys of homeownership any more than you do.

Yet, to be sure, owning a home is a different experience for military families. For instance, if a military husband wants to eventually lay tile over the concrete floor on the porch in spite of his wife's most sincere wishes otherwise, he has to begin said project as soon as possible. Preferably the day after he moves in. Military families get one night of rest. The next day, a mad dash begins to accomplish everything they've dreamed of for their new home because they are now one day closer to being relocated. In this way, military homeowners can not be procrastinating homeowners.

Admittedly, some of our experiences as military homebuyers might be unique to the lifestyle, but I think most of what we've learned along the way applies to civilians as well. With that in mind, here are the four tenets that Dustin and I follow when Uncle Sam has us in the market for a new home.

1. Always find the house with the best lawn. Then buy something else as far away as possible.

The easiest way to have a perfect yard is to live on the other side of the neighborhood from the guy who has the best yard. Staying away from the competition makes it much easier to look at your yard filled with crab grass and patches of brown and say, "Yep, looks good to me."

2. When choosing an area in which to live, it's a good idea to consider what kind of neighbors you will have and whether or not they will let you use their pool.

It's not the pool that matters; it's the invitation. Good neighbors don't just have pools; Good neighbors invite you to use their pool. This is especially handy for military families who have only two years to wait around for a contractor to build them their own pool.

3. A house with green shag carpet and orange linoleum better have something in its favor, like a good neighbor with a pool.

It's fun to fantasize about remodeling a house, even more fun to live in a house you like. If time and money are of the essence, don't kid yourself about how quickly (usually, just in time for the next homeowners to appreciate it) offensive carpet can be replaced.

4. By some phenomenon that few understand, your commute to work will not get shorter over time. It will only get longer.

I'm Just Saying…

"A forty-minute commute isn't that bad," you might be tempted to say, thinking in the back of your head that it will actually feel shorter if traffic is moving. However, science tells us that commutes only grow longer and more frustrating with time. Plus, traffic is seldom moving. Then again, if this house has good neighbors with a pool and brown grass, well then, the drive just might be worth it.

Transitional Delirium

This fall, my husband and I relocated from Jacksonville (affectionately known as "Jax"), Fla., to Pensacola. We lived in Jacksonville for three years, and leaving was torture.

Lucky for me though, this past weekend I realized that Kristi, one of my best friends from Jax, works at the local supermarket. I saw her there on Saturday. On Tuesday, I saw Sally's red Acura driving up Highway 90, and I'm pretty sure I saw Darcy eating at a deli downtown on Friday. My old neighbors, Tom and Michelle, live up the road—I see them walking their dog each night—and sure enough, the same policeman who gave me parking tickets in Jax apparently relocated to Pensacola, too.

Did all these people really follow me to Pensacola?

Of course not. I'm merely suffering from a condition I like to call "Transitional Delirium." It's an annoying affliction especially prevalent in the military, where families move often. Some common symptoms include wandering aimlessly through discount stores and forgetting where you parked your car; beginning every sentence with, "Well, back in _____ [insert the name of your previous home]"; thinking everything reminds you of people and places you used to know; and having frequent false-sightings of your old friends.

I'm pretty sure this delirium is the brain's way of easing the transition from one place to the next. Because your old friends and favorite places are so familiar and comfortable, your subconscious tries to find similarities between them and your new surroundings. If you're not careful, however, you might begin to think that your new friend who looks just like your old neighbor actually *is the old* neighbor. Calling people the wrong name is a common side effect of Transitional Delirium.

Humans suffering from this disorder are also known to call restaurants, shopping malls and streets by the wrong name. These people, by the way, should not be allowed in any discount store such as Target or Wal-Mart. All of these stores, no matter what city you're in, look eerily the same. Stick me in the middle of any Target in any town, and I'd have no idea what part of the country I'm in. They must use a master blueprint for all the stores, and this creates a lot of disorientation for the delirium-afflicted individual. These individuals walk out of the store and say, "Woa! For a minute there I thought I was at the Wal-Mart on San Jose Blvd. in Jacksonville! So where did I park my car anyway?"

Besides name-confusion and aimless wandering, however, it is relatively easy to spot those suffering from Transitional Delirium. They can frequently be found at parties saying things like, "Where we used to live ...," and comparing everything from the condition of the roads to the price of gas between their old home and the new one.

Acquaintances of these people sometimes get the feeling that the afflicted would rather be back in their old home, with their old friends. And sometimes this is true. More often than not, however, it just takes time for the delirium to run its course, and for the person to begin enjoying their new surroundings.

If you find, however, that you have been living in a new place for more than six months and you're still referring to the hamburger joint down the street as, "that place up the road that can't compare to the restaurant we used to go to," then you may have progressed to a more serious condition known as "Homesickness." This can be even more debilitating than the delirium, and left untreated, Homesickness can threaten any hope you might have of adjusting to your new residence. Immediate professional attention is recommended.

If you think you or someone you love might be suffering from Transitional Delirium and/or Homesickness, I urge you to find support. And I know the name of a great doctor who can help. Oh, but wait, he's ... um, back in Jax. You know, where I used to live.

Short-Timer Military Wives Have Nothing To Lose

A curious thing happens to a military wife when she knows her family will relocate soon. I liken it to the last glass of wine, the one that makes you go from the woman who would never sing "Sweet Home Alabama" in public to the woman who requests it at a bar and then shushes everyone so that they can hear her sing it. An impending move causes military wives to do things they might regret later, but it doesn't matter because they will already be gone by then.

Before we get to that, however, let's back up a bit and define "soon." Experienced military wives probably read the first sentence of this column and chuckled. "Aren't we all moving 'soon'?" they might have said. "Aren't we living in a constant state of 'moving soon'?"

While it's true that most military wives suffer from a lingering sense of temporariness no matter how long (another word that could stand clarification) their loved one's orders may be, something changes once moving is imminent.

My mom, a military wife of more than thirty years, lived in the same city for the last twenty-five years of my dad's career. It was an anomaly understood only by my dad's various detailers. Even so, due solely to the fact that Mom was a "military wife," she lived in constant fear of the next move, which actually never came. So it's fair to say that military wives are always "moving soon," even when they don't move for decades or more, but once the service member has orders in his hands and the date and location of the next move is, in theory, final, that is when the military wife officially becomes a "short-timer."

I had forgotten about this phenomenon of military life (perhaps because we've been at our current duty station for going on five years now), until I embarrassed myself at my son's tee-ball game by confronting the opposing coach about his yelling insults at the children.

"I'm so embarrassed," I said more than once the next day.

"Ah, don't worry about it," my friend Beth, a military wife, said. "You're a short-timer now, aren't you? Heck, I only have eight weeks left here; I'm liable to cause all kinds of trouble before then."

Short-timer military wives have been known to do many things in the weeks leading up to their moves. Chewing out a tee-ball coach is probably the least of them. Shore-timers have dramatically and abruptly quit jobs, sunbathed on the driveway (even if they shouldn't wear a bikini in public), yelled at principals, and told their neighbors what they really think about the pink flamingoes in their yard.

When my husband and I were leaving our last duty station, I finally got up the nerve to confront the teenagers one house away who threw wild parties when their father was out of town. Out into the driveway I went in my flannel pajamas, traipsed across the wet yard, and told the teens, who were standing on their father's driveway smoking and drinking, "If you don't all disappear in fifteen minutes, I'm calling the cops!"

"Go home, lady," one of them yelled back and kicked an empty beer can at me.

Me, a "lady"? It sounded so old, so matronly. Sure, I was standing in the grass in pajamas that looked like my grandfather's, but I was only 25 years old at the time. Embarrassed and more than a little deflated, I went back inside to my husband who was asleep and didn't care. I was mad that I didn't stick up for myself, and even more mad that I didn't actually call the cops. But mostly, I was mad that the teenagers had *always made me feel that way*.

About a week later, after my husband had his official orders to change duty stations, I was pulling weeds in the yard when the teenagers drove by in a beat-up truck. They yelled out their window and called me a name that can't be printed here.

But at least it wasn't "Lady."

I stood up, waved my shovel in the air, and yelled, "A $#%#$, huh? Now that's more like it!"

The next night, the teenagers had a party. I called the police.

It is both liberating and anxiety-provoking to leave a place that has become familiar. Emotions run high, and sometimes, inhibitions take a back seat.

Which is to say, if you want to know what a military wife really thinks, wait until her husband has orders to move. Or give her another glass of wine. Whichever.

You Put *What* On Our List?

On February 28th, Dustin had been home from work for several hours when he suddenly said quite casually, "Oh, did I tell you that they [they always means the "military" in sentences that begin like this] added Bangor, Maine, to our list of 'options' for my next duty station?" (I put options in quotations because the word wrongly implies that we have any perceivable control over the situation, which I'm about to prove.)

For months we had been waiting to find out about Dustin's next set of orders. We have been in Pensacola, Fla., for going on five years now. Many of our friends and family (perhaps even you) had begun to forget that Dustin is in the Navy. It just didn't make sense that we could stay in one place for so long, even if the actual reason was that Dustin had served as an instructor pilot for fixed-wing aircraft before switching to instruct in the helicopters.

I've lived the last two years waiting for the other shoe—er, flight boot—to drop, either with Dustin being sent on an IA (officially "Individual Augmentation," but might also be described as an inside sort of "draft") to Iraq, or orders to Guam. I was always careful not to write about our exact location, lest the powers that be finally realize we had become so comfortable here in Florida, we were actually seeing trees that we had planted grow and bloom. I worried that they (meaning "the military" again) might say, "What's Smiley still doing in Pensacola? Let's send that guy to Diego Garcia."

We've had it good for so long, we knew our time was about to come. The military likes to keep its people in a state of alternating between "this stinks" and "aren't we lucky?" I think it's part of their retention plan, but it feels more like playing the slot machines in Vegas.

It was a long, stressful period waiting for the list of places Dustin might be sent next. Especially because we knew it could literally be anywhere there is a Reserve Center. (Dustin's next job will be Commanding Officer of a Reserve Center.) When the list of "options" (there's that word again) finally came out, it was like Uncle Sam had chucked a handful of darts at the map. Our "options" were in three of the four corners of the country, and many places in between. But none of the options were extreme or unusual. There was Everett, Wash.; Columbus, Ga.; Allentown, Pa.; and places in Texas. We ranked our options, as suggested by the detailer, in order of preference from 1-6.

As of February 28th, however, I thought our list was still in the rough stages and had not been given to the detailer. So when Dustin mentioned Bangor, Maine, being added as an option at the last minute, I said, "Before you turn in the list, let's look at it one more time together and make sure we are still in agreement."

Dustin said, "Um, yeah, well...I kind of already turned in the list today."

"You *what*? Before or after you heard about Bangor?" (At this point, Bangor was, in my mind, a city buried under snow and ice, and as foreign to me as anyplace overseas.)

"Don't worry, I put Bangor number 7 of 7, so there's very little chance we'll be sent there," he said.

Right then, Dustin had sealed his fate as the cause of all my problems should the official orders not be to our liking. I would always be able to say, "If only you had let me see the list one more time before you turned it in..."

On April Fool's Day (of course!), Dustin came home, pulled out a chair and said, "I think you should sit down for this."

"We're going to the west coast again, aren't we?"

Dustin twisted up his face and smiled apologetically. "The boys have always wanted to see snow, right?" he said.

Yep, we're going to Bangor, Maine, the city we fought over that day when I found out that Dustin had turned in the "final" list without showing it to me first; the city Dustin threw onto the list before I even knew it existed as an "option," the city I have been using during the weeks since then to antagonize Dustin ("You're going to be awfully cold in Maine, Dustin." "When you're shoveling 20-feet of snow, will you think about us here in Florida?").

However, after a lot of crying and wondering if this could be reasonable grounds for divorce, I have come to a place of acceptance, and yes, even uncontainable excitement about the adventures that await us in Bangor. Mainly: (1) Stephen King lives there, and (2) I won't have to wear a bathing suit. But also: skiing, Portland, Brunswick, L.L. Bean, Moosehead Lake, Acadia National Park, trips to Canada, trips to Boston, and of course, throwing snowballs at Dustin.

I think Uncle Sam is having a very good laugh at this. Or maybe Dustin's detailer. Either one.

Garage Sale Is The Price We Pay

In an effort to make our house look a little less "lived in" (the words of our real estate agent), Dustin and I have spent the last week buried beneath piles of old clothes, still unused wedding gifts, and toys that are missing essential parts. Why we never got rid of these things before now, I do not know. We've also cleaned baseboards, painted rooms, mopped floors, and hidden personal items—again, on the advice of our agent—like Tucks medicated pads and contraceptive devices.

In preparation for the total strangers who will tour it and hopefully purchase it, our house is now cleaner and more organized than it ever has been for our visiting relatives, or even us.

But all the unwanted stuff that we cleaned out had to go somewhere. It wouldn't just evaporate, even though I prayed that it would. So it ended up in our garage.

"We need to have a garage sale," I told Dustin.

The look of horror on his face was similar to the one he had several years ago when I told him that our then dog (she has since gone to live with another family) dug up an entire tree in the backyard of our previous house, and dragged it, by her teeth, out to the golf course.

Dustin can't think of many things more degrading than hawking unwanted items on the driveway at an ungodly hour. You can take a perfectly good crockpot, slap a garage-sale sticker on it and set it on the concrete, and instantly, it looks like junk. What's worse than that, however, is watching strangers pick through your belongings, things you cared about two years ago but now have a $1.00-sticker on them, and wondering if they think it's weird that you have a book titled "How to Massage Your Cat."

Then, as if it were a sign from above (or, at least, from the president of the Homeowners' Association down the street), a newsletter arrived in our mailbox announcing the neighborhood's yearly community garage sale.

We took items out to the driveway quickly that morning while the kids still slept. We had to hurry before they saw us selling their T-Rex Mountain (the one they never play with) and Star Wars Attacktix (the ones that could take an eye out). By the time the boys woke up, our driveway looked like the attic and playroom had thrown up on it. The sun had barely poked out from behind the trees before our first customer arrived.

"How much for this stuffed duck?" they asked.

"Oh, I don't know. How about a dollar?" I said.

"A dollar? Are you kidding?"

"OK, 50 cents then?"

"Make it 10 cents and you've got a deal."

The buyer walked away with my son's duck flung over his shoulder. I had ten cents in my pocket and not one ounce of hope for all our other belongings that now seemed unfairly cheapened by the round, colorful price tags imposed on them. I was tempted to yell after the customer, "Oh yeah, well I was just going to throw that away anyhow!"

Several minutes later, a woman and her son were shopping. The son wanted one of my son's toy airplanes.

"No, that's junk," the mom said. She blushed when she realized that I had heard. I smiled, as if to say, "It's OK, I know what you meant." But what I was really thinking was, "It's ALL junk, lady."

I let her son take the airplane for free.

By noon, we still had more than half of our items left to sell. We planned to give the rest to the Salvation Army. But loading everything and driving it downtown seemed like yet another giant hurdle to having our house look "less lived in."

So, Dustin said, "The next person who comes up, tell them, 'Everything is a dollar.' And I don't mean each thing a dollar; I mean everything—all of it—one dollar."

Our next customer didn't think that sounded like a fair deal. All they wanted was our blender. Dustin told them they could have the blender and everything else—even the bent measuring spoon—for one dollar.

We ended up giving them the blender for free.

"Time for Plan B," Dustin said. "How about we pay the next person one dollar to take all of this away."

A customer walked onto the driveway and peered into a box of old video tapes. "Can I give you $5.00 for this whole box," he asked.

"No, I'll pay *you* $5.00 to take all of this away," Dustin said.

The man turned to leave.

"How about $20.00?" Dustin yelled. "Twenty dollars, and we'll pay your gas."

We realized then that our agent was right. There is much to gain by organizing and cleaning a house to put it on the market. But there is also a significant price to pay, and it isn't as cheap as a garage sale.

Your Spouse's Detailer: The Ultimate Boogeyman

When Dustin mentions his "detailer" (aka: the person who has the power to find me a new zip code), I picture a large man hunched over his desk with cigar smoke swirling up toward a bare, flickering light bulb in the ceiling. He is something like the Godfather, and he's just as powerful and scary.

Of course, this is only my imagination. I may never know what my husband's detailer really looks like because detailers are as elusive as my neighbor's one-eyed cat that slinks around in the bushes, only popping out now and then when my back is turned. Why else do you think the military keeps these people in places like Millington, Tennessee? I've only heard of one couple who knew and eventually became friends with their detailer, and I'm not sure this wasn't "illegal" in the same way that one can never know the true identity of someone in the Witness Protection Program.

From a spouse's perspective, the detailer is the ultimate boogeyman. You never see his face, and you probably don't know his name, but on any given day, he could change the course of your life (or at least your address) for the next eighteen months.

The detailer might also be your husband's scapegoat: "Honey, what could I do? The detailer told me that an unaccompanied tour in Diego Garcia was the best option right now."

Dustin wants me to add here (possibly because he is currently up for new orders) that detailers try very hard to meet the needs and desires of the service members to which they are assigned. Indeed, Dustin's detailers have always been gracious enough to grant us all of our wishes and desires that suit Uncle Sam.

A service member's conversation with the detailer might go something like this:

Detailer: So, what did you have in mind for your next career move?

Service Member: We'd like to stay on the East Coast if possible.

Detailer: Did you say you love the weather in San Diego?

Service Member: Um, no. I mean, well, I do love the weather in San Diego, but what I said was that my wife really wants to stay—

Detailer: Great, so it's settled. We'll put you down for something in San Diego or Everett, Wash. Unless you'd like to go to Guam instead?

Service Member: Guam?

Detailer: Yeah, I'll get back to you on whether or not you want to go there.

After a conversation such as this, the service member is then left in the unfortunate position of playing mediator between his wife and the detailer when he gets home. He will begin this talk with something like, "So, I talked to my detailer today …," and visions of a big, scary man—or a one-eyed cat, whichever you prefer—will enter your thoughts. You know it's bad news if what comes out of your spouse's mouth next is any of the following:

"You always said you wanted to be adventurous, right?"

"When you said you like cold weather, how cold did you mean?"

"How far west does the 'East Coast' extend?"

"Living far away from my parents is a good thing, right? Would Iceland be far enough away from them?"

"I hear they have great schools in [insert your least desirable place to live here]."

"I saw an article about the best and worst places to live in America, and did you know that [city and state] wasn't one of the worst?"

"The good news is that we're all healthy and happy, and whatever happens next, we will do it together."

And the number one worst way your husband could begin the conversation?

"How fast do you think we could sell this house?"

Eventually, you will begin to cry or hyperventilate, at which point your husband will say, "Before you get upset, let me talk to the detailer again tomorrow." This is only to buy himself more time.

I'm Just Saying...

Husbands never call their detailers the next day and say, "My wife cried when I told her about [city and state]. Do you think we could work out something else?" No, he will call the detailer and say, "My wife is onboard to do whatever the military asks of us."

None the wiser, when you get orders to [undesirable city and state], you will hate that big, mean, scary detailer even more for not listening to your requests as relayed (or so you think) by your spouse. And your husband will just smile and say, "Don't worry. The detailer promised that my next set of orders will be whatever we want that makes Uncle Sam happy."

The Military

Military Life:

WHAT WE WISH CIVILIANS KNEW.

What Not To Say, Part I

As troops continue to deploy for the war in Iraq, neighbors, teachers and friends struggle with what to say to the spouses left behind. And just as people unknowingly make insensitive remarks ("It's for the best," and "Everything happens for a reason") after the death of a loved one, people also say irritating things to military spouses.

One of the most common offenses goes something like this: "I can't believe my husband will be away on business all weekend!" Or "I'm so disappointed, my husband had to work on our anniversary." This rubs military spouses the wrong way because our loved one's absences can be measured in months, not weekends, and they're usually five-six time zones away on our anniversary, birthday, Christmas, Thanksgiving, and the day that our son says his first word. Military spouses learn to appreciate modified holidays, like Christmas in July, and to view "weekend business trips" not as an unbearable tragedy, but rather, as a welcomed vacation from whiskers in the sink and Athlete's Foot powder on the tile floor.

Even so, everything is still relative. For the wife whose husband usually doesn't leave, a weekend business trip is a big deal. So it's not that military spouses want sympathy. We just want validation. We want our suffering to be a reminder for others to appreciate what they have. As long as a civilian wife appreciates her husband 99 percent of the time while ours are deployed, we can hold fast to the idea that military families sacrifice so others don't have to.

Maybe now you're thinking, "Well, I've heard military wives joke about finding a ship for their husband to sail away on when he's been home too long! *They* aren't always so appreciative!" This is absolutely true, if not totally confusing. When our husbands are deployed, we desire sensitivity from civilian families. Talk to us three months post-deployment, however, and we're more than happy to gripe about the way our husband smacks his lips when he's eating cereal. This is because no one can live in a perpetual state of bliss and idealism. There is an end to every honeymoon.

Remember after 9/11 when everyone was remarkably kind and patient with one another? Remember how long it took most of us to feel irritated again about little things like a car going too slow on the interstate? Humans simply can not maintain such a heightened state of appreciation. Life goes on. Someone drives with their blinker on. The dog digs up the garden. And slowly, we slip back into being mere mortals who are often flippant, despite the fact that we once claimed we'd never take our husband (freedom, health, safety) for granted.

When our husbands are deployed, we military wives feel a great sense of appreciation and perspective. But it doesn't take long (usually before the seabag is unpacked) for us to fall from that moral pedestal and join other humans who get mad about dirty laundry on the bathroom floor.

Of course, these peaks and valleys needn't be unique to military lives. Have you ever seen a quadriplegic on "Oprah" and silently vowed never to take your arms and legs for granted, only to catch yourself bothered by a nasty mosquito bite on your toe three hours later?

Getting back to the first analogy about a grieving widow: she will eventually see the "reasons" and "blessings" in her circumstance, but she probably isn't ready to hear about it at the funeral. A year later, she might be able to laugh about her husband's awful snoring, but she isn't ready for jokes right now.

In the same way, a military wife might not feel sympathy for your husband's weekend trip when her husband is halfway around the world for the next six months. But she might want you to laugh and give a knowing nod when she calls her husband a doofus nine months later.

My best advice to civilians: stay patient and understanding, and when in doubt, just say, "thank you for your sacrifice."

Next week: "Has your three-year old learned the alphabet yet?" and other questions military wives don't care to answer when they're busy surviving deployment.

What Not To Say, Part II

When Dustin's first deployment was extended in the wake of the terrorist attacks on September 11, 2001, I was at home with an eleven-month-old baby (Ford) and recovering from a serious case of Postpartum Depression. Around this same time, someone asked if I had considered joining the local Mommy and Me gymnastics group. I looked at them and laughed. Because frankly, I didn't have time to worry about my son's tumbling skills.

My mom, a Navy wife for thirty years, actually has a term to describe this type of deployment parenting. She calls it "Survival Mode." Her theory is that when a military wife and mother is overwhelmed with single-parenting, home repairs, finances, plus her own career during her spouse's deployment, sometimes she might not also have time to teach her toddler French. Making priorities becomes the order of the day, and basically, anything that doesn't involve avoiding bankruptcy or managing a hot dinner now and then simply isn't at the top of the list.

During my first deployments as a military wife, I worried excessively about the fact that my neighbor's son ate only homemade apple sauce and so far mine just liked to spit canned fruits and vegetables across the kitchen.

"You don't have time to worry about homemade apple sauce," Mom told me over the phone. "You're in survival mode now."

A military wife knows she is in survival mode when frozen pizzas and waffles tumble out of the freezer every time she opens the door. She knows she is in survival mode when a good day is defined by the amount of crayons her child has eaten. She knows she is in survival mode when studies claiming that television is bad for children seem like pranks. And she knows she is in survival mode when Mommy and Me seems like a hysterical idea, considering she hasn't done laundry in two weeks.

I have vivid memories of my mom cleaning toilets at odd hours of the night during my dad's many deployments. I remember her throwing her hands up in the air when my teenage brothers left to go surfing in the middle of a storm. And I remember her falling asleep on a small, wooden children's chair next to my bed when I was afraid of the dark and didn't want to be in my room alone.

Back then, Mom often seemed crazy. She looked tired and frazzled. Sometimes I thought she wasn't coping very well. I know now that she was merely in survival mode. By the time my dad had 11 years of sea time under his belt, Mom had learned that she could only hold herself to a certain, reasonable standard while he was away. She couldn't be a perfect parent. Sometimes she couldn't even strive for "great." She was just hoping for "good enough." We were fed, we went to school everyday, and we were happy. So what if we didn't learn a foreign language or eat organic vegetables?

All this is not to say that military wives aren't strong and capable. Quite the opposite. Military wives are strong *because* they know their limits and make priorities. They are capable because they recognize that they can't do it all.

So what does this mean for civilian friends and neighbors and what they should or should not say to a military wife?

Don't question why her children's bikes and dump trucks are scattered all across the lawn at eight o'clock at night. She's probably too busy making frozen pizzas to clean up the yard.

Don't snicker because her son hasn't had a haircut in four weeks and wispy strands stick up in the back. If she had time to cut his hair, she wouldn't have time to do the laundry.

And please, for the love of all that is good, unless she offers otherwise, never ask if her preschooler knows his alphabet, takes gymnastics or knows French.

When your military-wife friend isn't busy surviving, she'll work on being perfect. Her children might not eat all the right things, and her house might be a mess, but I can promise you this, to the family she takes care of, that military wife in survival mode is the closest thing to Wonder Woman that they'll ever see.

What Not To Say, Part III

For the past two weeks, we've been discussing "what not to say to a military wife." We've learned that civilians in the presence of a "deployment widow" should not lament their spouse's weekend business trip, and women everywhere should cut military wives some slack when they are in "Survival Mode" (aka "I don't have time to teach my toddler French because I'm busy heating up frozen fish sticks.") We will close this three-week series with a hodgepodge of irritating questions that don't fit underneath one umbrella theme.

"Six months is such a long time! How do you do it?"

First of all, we've looked at the calendar. We know exactly how long six months is. What's more, we know that six months actually feels longer than it looks. When people remind military wives about the length of time, it is like someone telling a person with a broken leg, "Wow, that must have hurt." Stating the obvious is irritating. Assume that if, for some reason, a military wife doesn't know how long six months is, it would be unkind of you to teach her.

It is the second part of this statement, however, that troubles many military wives the most. When our spouses are on deployment, we get into a groove. We can't stop to think about our reality too long, or it will seem even more daunting. We have children to take care of and businesses to run, so giving up isn't an option.

I compare it to childbirth. If women focused on the pain and what's actually happening to their body during labor, we'd need someone to hit us over the head with a 2-by-4 before we went into the delivery room. We don't have an option; the baby is coming. So we go into a haze-like state, where we persevere and do what needs to be done. It's only later that we stop and say, "How did I do that?"

Don't break a military wife's concentration. Don't make her stop and wonder how she's "doing it." But if you dare to go there anyway, and you ask, "How do you do it?" don't be surprised if she snaps, "Do I have another choice?"

"Will he be able to come home when you have the baby?"

No. He also won't be able to come home when I have the flu, when the dog dies, or when our son has his tonsils taken out. We military spouses have worked hard to put these thoughts out of our minds. We've stopped wishing for life's little moments to be placed on pause while our husband's are away.

Civilians can't be totally blamed for their lack of awareness, however. Military families are partly at fault when we loosely refer to deployments as "cruises" and we talk about the jewelry and other goodies our spouses buy in foreign ports. Often I fear, we've made deployments sound like a vacation. So let me just make this clear for civilians once and for all: tonsils, childbirth, and even funerals almost always take a backseat to Uncle Sam. So don't ask.

"How do you feel about the war?"

Many military spouses despise this question when their loved one is deployed for one simple reason: it doesn't matter. We can wax philosophical about the politics of war, but it doesn't change our reality or make it any easier. Our spouses are gone, and no one asked for their opinion, much less ours. It's their job to serve the country, and we've learned to not only accept that fact, but also to separate it from politics. No political, moral or ethical epiphany will bring our spouses home, so we don't dwell on the "right" and "wrong" of the situation.

We're just focused on doing our part—supporting our husbands —and for that, you can never go wrong by simply saying "thank you."

Do Soldiers Receive Obscene Amenities?

I'm a little late weighing in on William Arkin's Washington Post.com commentary, "The Troops Also Need to Support the American People" (January 30, 2007), but I have good reason. For the last few weeks I've been searching for all those "obscene amenities" and other luxuries of military life to which Arkin alluded. Here's what I found.

The troops have Internet access

Yes, it's true. Most of the troops stationed in Iraq have Internet access. Are they granted this "luxury" to look up porn or waste time that they don't have (many of them are working 16-hour days, seven days a week)? No. Basically, what Internet access means to the troops is the ability to connect with their families back home. Exchanging email with loved ones and receiving instant pictures of one's children provides enormous morale for the men and women stationed overseas. Furthermore, in an era when many people (Arkin included, I'm sure) are connected 24/7 with cell phones, Blackberries and high-speed Internet, can we say that giving email capabilities to the troops is excessive or obscene? By today's standards, most people consider connectivity a basic necessity, similar to having a phone installed in your home.

The troops receive special treats

Sometimes men and women stationed overseas receive special treats. Are we talking about prime rib prepared by Wolfgang Puck? No. Usually the "treat" is a token item to remind the service members of home. For example, just recently some troops enjoyed a dish of Baskin Robbins ice cream. Perhaps this seems "obscene" and excessive to Arkin. What he should remember, however, is that for many stationed overseas, mealtime is the only highlight of their day. They're living in crammed quarters and working long hours under strenuous conditions. If going to the Mess Hall for a bowl of ice cream gives them something to look forward to, I'm glad my tax dollars can provide it. I'm going to go out on a limb here and say that Arkin probably isn't living off peanut butter and jelly and canned soup either.

Military families have "free" healthcare

Let's define "free." When something is free, you pay nothing for it. Give nothing, get something. Very few things in life are truly free, least of all military benefits, such as healthcare, for which service members sacrifice more than many civilians can imagine. No, we don't pay money for healthcare. We pay with other intangible things far more important than money. We "pay" when our spouse is halfway across the world for their son's birth. We "pay" when our spouse misses their child's first smile, first step and first word. And ultimately, we "pay" when one day our spouse does not come home from Iraq. If Arkin had to "pay" for healthcare in this way, I wonder if he would consider it "free."

Military families receive a decent wage

"Decent" is such a relative term, but for what it's worth, let me show you the realities of military pay, and you can decide for yourself what's "decent." Assume that an E-3 with two years of service is stationed overseas, receiving basic pay (about $1458/month), hazardous duty pay (about $150/month), sea pay (about $100/month) and a housing allowance (about $407/month, depending on the area of the country in which that member is officially stationed). Now let's assume this E-3 is working 30 days a month, averaging 10 working hours each day (a gross underestimation considering our theoretical E-3 is deployed). When you take all of the above into account and break it down into an hourly wage, the E-3 is making $7.05 an hour. Decent?

Military families receive "free" housing

There's that little word "free" again. Some consider our benefits a perk of military life, but I can assure you that the sacrifices far outweigh them. It isn't even a close call. The cinderblock homes we call "base housing" are relatively decent and sufficient, but they're hardly excessive. Arkin's probably visited hotels nicer than some base housing.

And I haven't even mentioned that a soldier making $7.00 an hour while his family lives in base housing might eat a cup of ice cream one night and then die for our freedom the next day.

So where are all these obscene amenities? I haven't a clue. Perhaps Mr. Arkin should enlist and help us find them.

Sorry, Mayer, Service Members Don't Want To Wait

John Mayer's new single, "Waiting on the World to Change," is seriously flawed.

And I don't mean musically.

Each time I hear the song on the radio, it fills me with dread and sadness, but mostly, despair.

As a military wife, I specifically take issue with Mayer's fourth verse, which suggests that if the government had only brought home the troops long ago, service men and women "would have never missed a Christmas/no more ribbons on the door." If Mayer knows of some secret guarantee that military families will never be separated again after the war in Iraq ends, I wish he'd share it with the rest of us. In all the 30 years that I've been a military family member, I've never known the military to offer any guarantees.

So I'll tell Mayer something I do know: Service members deploy—missing Christmases, Thanksgivings, births, deaths and anniversaries—war or no war. And what's more, they do it when no one else is watching, when their job isn't front-page news. An end to the war in Iraq does not mean an end to missed Christmases, and therefore, it should not mean an end to "ribbons on the door."

This notion that military sacrifices cease at the end of a conflict is seriously misguided. No one knows that better than service members and their families. By the time I was 22-years-old, my Navy dad had been deployed off and on for a total of 11 years. In that time, there were many missed Christmases and birthdays—Dad even missed my birth—but only a small percentage of absences could be blamed on a war or conflict. Most deployments were simply "part of the job."

Aircraft carriers and troops don't stay home until the world needs them. They are constantly rotating in and out of deployment schedules, and I've never known Uncle Sam to alter his timeline based on Christmas (or births, deaths and anniversaries). Like a fireman who goes to work on Christmas Eve, or a doctor who is on-call at Thanksgiving, there is no break for the military's watch.

But what about the reservist?

It's true that what's normal for active-duty military is unusual for reservists and their families. The reservists' lives have been turned upside down by the war. But let's not forget that reservists, like their active-duty counterparts, volunteered for the position they serve. Also, like active-duty service men and women, reservists arrived at that decision by one discernible characteristic that sets apart all who work in a helping profession: a commitment to serve.

This brings me to the most disturbing part of Mayer's song—the refrain. Mayer is "waiting" (and waiting and waiting and waiting) "on the world to change." He mentions feeling helpless when he's "standing at a distance." His solution? Keep on waiting. All that waiting on the sidelines strikes me as both depressing and apathetic.

Interestingly, however, the very people who aren't merely "waiting," are the men and women in uniform, the men and women who are missing Christmas, the men and women we honor and remember with a ribbon on the door. They are neither "standing at a distance" nor passively hoping for change. Instead, they are actively doing their part to make a difference. And if you asked them, most service members would say that missed holidays are a necessary, albeit difficult, reality to accomplish their goals.

So my fear is that "Waiting on the World to Change" is spreading the wrong message. First, it furthers some people's belief that military men and women are passive robots who begrudgingly carry out the needs of the Department of Defense, instead of what they are: people who made an active commitment to serve, no matter the sacrifices. And second, Mayer's song offers little suggestions, besides waiting, of how young people today might make a difference in the world. From the lyrics, you'd think we're all helpless and desperate, waiting for someone else to make the world better.

Yet anyone who believes that hasn't met the men and women of the armed services. Because if they had, they would know, service members don't want to wait with Mayer. They want to be doing. And if that means missing Christmas, they will endure so that Mayer and others can continue to wait ... in peace.

But Seriously:

I'M JUST SAYING…

Christmas Is A Time To Remember Those Still Deployed

Last week I decorated for Christmas, which is my favorite thing to do all year. It's even better than eating candy leftover from Halloween. Nothing brings out the child in me more than tying a red bow on a wreath and singing "Holly, Jolly Christmas." Just give me a sugar cookie cut in the shape of Rudolph and I'm a happy girl.

Ironically, however, besides being giddy over twinkling lights and dancing Santa Clauses, I'm also quite meticulous when it comes to holiday decorations. Call me crazy, but when I'm stringing 300 lights across the bushes of our lawn, I like to do it with some sort of strategy.

This goes against every disorganized fiber of my husband's being, and therefore, I am the designated light-decorator in our home.

As part of my plan for organized, happy decorating, I put a great deal of thought into how I disassemble and store our trimmings the year before. With patience and care, I put away the strands of lights each January.

Last Christmas, however, I made the mistake of allowing my husband to take down the lights. Yes, he was doing me a favor and I shouldn't complain, but when he dumped on the floor four strands of miniature white lights (wound tightly into a ball), I couldn't help but be upset.

For the sake of harmony, I tried to undo the mess of chords in silence. Eventually I gave up, shoved the lights into their box and said to my husband, "Oh forget it, I'll just pack them away and save that argument for next year!"

Which brings us to last week.

My festive jingle-bell-mood couldn't easily be sabotaged ... until I went outside to dangle lights from the trees.

My first clue should have been the way the box of lights was bulging and looked so unlike my usual careful packing. But no, whistling and happy, I was totally unprepared for what was waiting there when I opened the lid. When I saw it—a giant wad of twisted, tangled white lights—I shrieked in horror. Instantly, my holiday smile turned into the dreadful disapproving-wife frown.

Not to spoil the Christmas festivities, however, I attempted to untie the lights myself. With each knot, I became more frustrated and angry. I threw the mess onto the pavement, ran inside and yelled to my husband, "Dustin, I'm ready for that argument now!"

The cheerful mood of the Smiley house that day quickly dissolved into a battle of, "If you hadn't been so rushed last year putting these away, we wouldn't be untangling them now," and "If you don't like the way I do it, Sarah, why don't you do them yourself next time!"

We retreated to our own separate corners of the house to pout about the day's activities.

Then, alone in my room, I saw a news clip about a helicopter crash in Iraq that killed six Marines, and my heart began to change. One year ago, my husband was gearing up to leave for Operation Enduring Freedom. His squadron left nearly four months earlier than was planned, and we had no idea when they'd be back.

For many reasons, it was one of the worst deployments I've ever been through. Last Christmas, I didn't know what the year would hold for my family or if we'd all be together for the 2004 holiday season.

What was an unrealized potential for me, however, is a reality for thousands of families who are missing service-member loved ones this Christmas.

Last year, I didn't know if my husband would be here; this year I'm yelling at him for his light-winding abilities. How could I be so ungrateful?

This month, thousands of military families will bear the pain of a holiday spent apart. Some will be missing soldiers and sailors deployed overseas. Many will be missing those who have died. And still others will be celebrating the season under the impending gloom of an upcoming deployment.

For those of us who will have our families together this season, we should remember to be grateful. We must never forget our fellow military friends and family who will be celebrating alone or across the miles.

When you picture a soldier spending Christmas Day in a tent in the desert so that we can have our freedom, it makes tangled lights seem a little trivial, doesn't it?

Honoring Astronauts, Veterans At Space Center

We were visiting the Space Center just south of Houston, Texas, and adjacent to Johnson Space Center, so I envisioned something...well, something out of this world. I thought we'd see plasma televisions, computers and lighting like we've never witnessed before. I thought the building would be futuristic. I even imagined it being spherical, although I'm not sure why.

What we found at the Space Center was time travel of a different sort—straight to the 1960s.

"It just seems so ordinary," I kept saying to Dustin.

"What did you expect?" he wanted to know.

We boarded a tram that looked like it had been rescued from Disney's used-tram junk yard (this wasn't the monorail), and embarked on a tour of the actual base where astronauts train.

"The tour is one and a half hours," the guide said. "And there aren't any bathrooms."

I looked at Dustin.

"Is that too long?" he asked me.

Anything that lasts more than fifteen minutes is too long when you have three children—all under the age of seven, and one of them in diapers—along with you. But I could see that Dustin was as excited as a kid in a toy shop to be getting on that tram bound for the real-life space center, so the five of us piled into a tight row with cracked plastic seats, and I hoped that the baby would not dirty his diaper.

"I'm surprised they don't have a sophisticated monorail or

something," I whispered to Dustin. But he wasn't listening. He and my other three boys wanted to see rockets and spaceships.

The base looked oddly familiar even though I had never been there before. The buildings were plain and square. Plaques that looked more functional than they did aesthetic were on the sides of each building to mark their fancy address: "Building 2," Building 3," etc. Evidence of utilities—pipes, wiring, electrical boxes—were peppered on the sides of the street and attached to the buildings like aggressive spaghetti. Steam billowed out of holes in the ground. And then I realized why everything seemed so familiar: The Johnson Space Center looked like every other military base I've ever been to in my life. It was plain, functional, and lacking all comforts. It looked like it was designed by men. Based solely on first appearances, you'd never believe a place such as this could put a man on the moon.

In one of the buildings, we saw where astronauts train to maneuver in the International Space Station. Giant mock-ups were crowded into a hangar several stories tall. There was even a simulator of the space shuttle. Now my kids were really amazed. They pressed their noses against the glass. I noticed a man, an employee, down below, walking between the modules. He was like a celebrity to us: someone who works at the actual space station!

But then, for reasons I don't know, I began to think about all the times I went with my Navy dad onto the aircraft carriers at Norfolk Naval Base. I have been on almost every aircraft carrier on the East Coast, and growing up, my visits to them were as insignificant to me as I imagine trips to an office building might be for a child whose dad is an accountant or lawyer. I had climbed ladders and gangplanks, walked around jets in the hangar, and once, before the ships were adjusted to accommodate women, I used the men's head. None of these things ever seemed unusual to me until I saw my dad's workplace through someone else's—a visiting relative or friend—eyes.

Now I watched the man at the space center and realized that he is not unlike you and me. He probably has a wife calling his cell phone to ask, "Will you be home for dinner tonight?" and a child who wants to know if Dad will be there for his school play. Yes, he might send men to the moon and beyond, but the man himself, and the place where he works, is just as normal—just as earthly—as anything else you've ever seen.

I'm Just Saying...

At the end of our tram ride, we passed a circular grove of trees that is a memorial to all the astronauts who have died on missions. It is a modest, humble memorial. Nothing flashy. You wouldn't even know it was there if someone didn't point it out. Just like the base surrounding it, the memorial was very much "of this world."

It seemed fitting then that we paused to honor the grove of trees on Memorial Day weekend. Because it's true that the astronauts, just like service members, have a mission that is incomprehensible to some, and yet the risks to both are entirely human. And that makes their sacrifice and their work all the more commendable.

Thoughts On The War In Iraq

Probably more than any other group of people, military spouses are schooled in the art of patience. We have learned to be flexible and to endure because we are married into a system that for all its structure is still quite unpredictable. We've learned to be prepared for short-notice moves, unexpected separations, and deployments that last longer than planned. We've grown used to long stretches of time when we can't speak to our spouses. And we've braced ourselves for the ultimate shock—an officer standing at our door.

So while the rest of the world debates the war in Iraq and grows impatient for the troops' return, we spouses wait patiently—tolerantly—because we know that the work our loved ones do can't be measured in 30-second sound bites and headlines that change with each coming day.

This is precisely what sets military families apart from the rest. I can't help but laugh when the media says that America is ready for the war to end so that our service members can return home to their families. Any military spouse knows an end to the war in Iraq doesn't necessarily mean an end to our loved one's sacrifices.

Serving in the military is my husband's job. The hardships his duty entails don't cease during peacetime. Yes, troops will come home when the war in Iraq has ended, but soon those troops will turn around and deploy again, maybe not to Iraq, and maybe not to a war, but they will deploy nonetheless.

When the active duty military members return from Iraq, they won't suddenly have 9-to-5 jobs and be around for all their children's birthdays again. To think otherwise is to be unaware of the daily sacrifices our military make on a continual basis.

Indeed, for the families waiting back home, there is infinitesimal difference between the sacrifices made during a wartime deployment and those made during one which is "routine." Yes, there is more stress and more to worry about when a loved one is deployed to a war, but in general, the lives of military spouses hasn't changed very much since before the war in Iraq began. I say this with caution, of course, because for the woman who has lost her husband in the war, life has certainly changed. But for the most part, this is our daily life. This is what our spouses do. The only difference today is that more people care, and there is increased attention from the media.

People in the media often ask me, "How many times has your husband deployed to a war?" and I dodge the question, not because I'm being elusive, but rather, I think it shouldn't matter. In fact, my husband has *only* deployed during war time. But does that make my sacrifices more relevant than my mother's, when her husband (my dad) had been at sea for a total of eleven years (most of them "routine") by the time they reached their 22nd wedding anniversary?

Just the other day, a reporter asked me, "Are you anxious for the war in Iraq to be over so that your husband doesn't have to deploy anymore?" I couldn't help it; I laughed. Out loud. Who says my husband won't deploy? If I've learned anything during my time as a military wife, it is this: nothing is guaranteed. The only way my husband won't deploy anymore is if he gets out of the military completely.

For military spouses, the cycle of deployments, missed holidays, lonely anniversaries, and long separations isn't governed by any war or what's being debated on CNN. It is as much a part of our daily living as weekend business trips and conference calls are to someone with a different career. It is part of the job description. And thank goodness, my husband has a job whether there is a war or not!

So don't have pity for us. Don't wish an end to the war for our sakes. Instead, have appreciation. Be in awe that service men and women of the United States are deployed every day of every year. War or no war. And their families are waiting month after month, during routine and wartime deployments alike. Remember that just as our service member counterparts have been trained for duty, we have been trained for patience. And that's something the rest of America could stand to learn as well.

Uncle Sam: Keeping Me Healthy AND Happy?

I take 100mg of Zoloft, an anti-depressant, every morning. Perhaps that is more than you wanted to know. Or maybe it is exactly what someone out there needed to hear. Despite the stigma surrounding anti-depressants, no thanks to Tom Cruise, I wouldn't start my day without them.

I began taking Zoloft almost seven years ago when I was suffering from a very bad case of postpartum depression. When I say "postpartum depression," I don't just mean that I was weepy and apprehensive. I mean that I was lying on the floor like a rag doll, crying for my mom to take care of the baby. It didn't help that Dustin was about to leave for his first six-month deployment.

Zoloft was a Godsend—a miracle, a wonder drug, a ... um, order from my doctor. I think his exact words were, "You need to get a grip on yourself," which is a whole other story, because obviously that was not the best approach. In any case, I started taking Zoloft, and Dustin in turn learned that he is a very big fan of the drug. He could leave for his deployment with a little less concern for me.

I've been taking Zoloft ever since. Yes, even through two subsequent pregnancies, and all three of my children are fine (unless you take into account the fact that one of them wears red briefs on the outside of his pants to look more like Superman, and the other one is proud to be called "Toot Master General").

The first time I was without Zoloft was last month when I was on vacation and my prescription ran out. Because I've been a military dependent my entire life, I have a child's understanding of medical insurance. I've always simply arrived at the hospital, given them my Social Security number, and magically, I received care. Same thing with medicine: I go to the pharmacy window, hand them my identification card, and presto, a brown bag is handed across the counter. There is no money involved. No paperwork. No questions.

So you can imagine my confusion when I went to the local civilian pharmacy and asked for a few pills, enough to get me home, and the whole thing turned into a hoop-jumping, paper-shuffling ordeal. "Your insurance won't pay for that," the pharmacist said. "The Navy hospital will have to call us, and we're not sure if they can call in a prescription out-of-state. You might have to get in touch with Tricare."

I stood there confused. "But don't I just show you this [holding up ID card], and you give me my medicine?"

Turns out it doesn't work that way on the outside. There is paperwork, phone calls, and ... money?

"Fine, I'll just buy a month's supply outright," I told the pharmacist. "Forget insurance and whatnot, just give me my Zoloft."

"Sure, that will be $107," he said.

Huh?

I couldn't afford that, so I bought three pills, enough to get me to the safety of my military surroundings, and it took all the cash I had in my wallet.

Walking out of the store, I had renewed appreciation for the military and my healthcare. Just as a child seldom understands the sacrifices of their parent, I never realized that the military has spent $107 on me every month for six years. I've never had to pay a thing. (Except that my active-duty husband has been gone much of that time, I've spent anniversaries and birthdays alone, and I've worried many nights that Dustin would not come home alive. "Payment" is such a relative thing.)

Uncle Sam: keeping yours truly healthy and happy for 31 years. I am both humbled and grateful.

Opting-Out Of Recruiters' Lists

Recently, I read an article in *USA TODAY* ("Some Opt-Out of Military Options," by Judy Keen, Nov. 4, 2006) that presented me with a major parenting and philosophical dilemma: Would I "hide" my children from military recruiters?

According to the article, parents of teenagers can opt out of a "No Child Left Behind" provision allowing schools to share their child's contact information with military recruiters. To some, recruiters are notorious for repeatedly calling and visiting high school students, encouraging them to enlist in the armed services. The Pentagon maintains that recruiters only desire the same information available to universities and corporations searching for new employees. From a parent's point-of-view, however, it's one thing for Microsoft to court your child, and quite another for the Pentagon to do so. In fact, there are entire websites with names like "Leave My Child Alone" and "Not Your Soldier" set up for parents concerned about such a thing. I could be wrong, but I've never seen a "Not Your Future CEO" help-site.

Some teenagers quoted in the *USA TODAY* article likened recruiters to telemarketeres who will stop at nothing to get what they want. Others conceded that recruiters aren't that bad and possibly no different than representatives from other organizations they run into at career fairs. The bottom line, however, is that the decision to give recruiters access to your child is ultimately in the hands of the parents. The method varies from school to school, but all offer some way for parents to take their child's contact information off the recruiters' list.

All of which made me wonder, will I opt-out my own children when the time comes?

I'm Just Saying...

I am a military wife, a military columnist and a military daughter. I've been affiliated with the military and its people in one way or another for more than 30 years. Yet still, my gut tells me that I'd probably choose to keep my boys away from military recruiters.

There, I've said it. And I feel much better now, thank you.

But before my military-family counterparts rush to blogs and message boards to harangue me, let me explain.

I'm not saying that I would forbid Ford and Owen from serving in the military. In fact, I'd never "forbid" my boys from anything except drugs, smoking, crime and marrying before they're 40. It's likely that my children will be interested in serving their country. Their father, their grandfathers, and most of their great-grandfathers all served in the armed services. It is as much a part of our family as eating cornbread-and-sausage dressing at Thanksgiving dinner.

Ironically however, it is that same intimate knowledge of military life that brings me to my decision about recruiters. Mainly, I know that serving in the military requires more dedication, sacrifice, and commitment than possibly any other profession. For all of the military's "perks" (education, travel, experience, training), there are many more sacrifices. One cannot join the military to "see the world" then change their mind when duty (namely, war) calls. It is foolish to enlist without giving serious consideration to the fact that someday you might be asked to make the ultimate sacrifice. When it comes to the needs of the country, the military doesn't care if you signed up "to get an education" or to "travel the globe." Your job is to answer the call—no questions asked.

Don't get me wrong, all of the above makes military men and women some of the most respectable and notable people in our country. But when my children make a decision to commit their life to something as binding and important as the military, do I want them to use information and input from a stranger?

My gut reaction is a resounding no.

I would be proud for either of my boys to serve in the military. I would admire their decision and support them in it. But I'd also want to give them all the facts first, and I wouldn't want a stranger to be a part of that discussion.

So would I "hide" Ford and Owen from military recruiters? Let's just say that when it comes to military service and sacrifice, I want that discussion to begin at home. I want it to begin with us.

For This Veteran, Every Day Is A Good Day

I was sitting in the lobby of the ophthalmology clinic at the Navy hospital in Pensacola, Fla., waiting for my pupils to dilate and wondering why I bother wearing mascara to these appointments, when an old man parked his wheelchair next to my seat. His left leg from the knee down was gone. He had tied his navy blue slacks in a knot to conceal what was left. We both looked at the television hanging from the ceiling above us, where Hillary Clinton and Barack Obama were in the middle of a debate about healthcare. Ironic, I thought.

"Ah, politics," I said and smiled over at my waiting-room companion.

Before he could respond, a nurse came around the corner to take him back for his appointment.

"How are you doing, Sir?" the nurse asked.

"Oh, I can't complain," he said as he wheeled his chair toward her.

I was already well acquainted with the nurse. She was the one with the magic drops and the space-age machine that would eventually take pictures of the back of my eyeball. For six weeks, I had been complaining about a bright light in my right eye. The ophthalmologist wanted to check for tears or a detachment. The spot was a major nuisance while I was reading, writing or driving. The nurse had heard all about it while she gave me my drops. So when the man said he couldn't complain, I smiled at him and said, "Don't worry, I've already complained enough for the both of us."

The man and nurse disappeared down the hall. I picked up a magazine to read, despite my growing pupils and the fact that the overhead light might as well have been a flood light.

A few minutes later, the man returned to wait with me while his pupils grew. The palms of his hands were covered in black dirt, and the musty smell of tobacco smoke drifted over from his flannel shirt.

"Nope, I can't complain," he said, picking up where we had left off.

"I've had this spot in my eye for weeks now and it's driving me crazy," I said.

The man nodded.

"I hate having my pupils dilated, and not being able to read while we wait here."

The man nodded again.

"Gosh, could that overhead light be any brighter?" I said. (Have I ever mentioned how bad I am at small talk?)

"When they found me in 'Nam, my eyeballs were sitting on top of my cheeks, still attached to the nerve," the man said. He wasn't looking at me. "They said I'd never see again. Took a bullet right through my forehead."

I looked at my lap shamefully. How could I have been so stupid to complain?

"The doctors still can't explain it," he said. "They thought I was blind for life. But sure enough, I can see you plain as day." Finally he turned his head to look at me. He smiled warmly. "Yes, today is a very good day, a very good day."

I couldn't forget that man for several days afterwards. Incidentally, our command had a casualty the same week. Someone's husband had not come home alive—kind of makes all the day's nuisances seem inconsequential. I was beginning to feel down on military life. What's the point, I wondered. Why risk all these lives when most of America doesn't even seem to care?

Then I remembered something else the man in the wheelchair had said: "For my country, I'd do it all again in a heartbeat. I was blind, and now I see."

As we mark the five-year anniversary of our involvement with Iraq, and while the politicians continue to fight over when to leave and who was right or wrong, let us all remember that at the end of the day, if a soldier has completed his mission and come home to his family alive, it is a very good day indeed. And while some of us gripe about long lines, slow traffic lights, and the high price of gas, there is a man with one leg who despite a bullet in his head and years lost to blindness, still can't complain. Neither should we.

Hat Picture Causes Controversy

Due to the recent amount of feedback I've received over the military cover (hat) I wear in my headshot, I think it's time to discuss "The Hat Picture" (as it is now affectionately known around the Smiley house).

On my webpage and next to my column in the newspapers, there is a picture of me wearing a Naval officer's cover. This photo—The Hat Picture—has created quite a stir with some readers. I've been told that I'm "disgracing the uniform" and that the picture is "appalling." Some newspapers in fact have chosen not to publish the headshot for fear of offending members of the military.

Let me back up now and tell you how this photo came to be. Actually, I expected this controversy the day I posed for the picture at a photo shoot with *Pensacola News Journal*. At first, I was against using the cover as a prop for my picture.

However, the photographer took dozens of shots that day (half with the hat and half without), and the deal was that I'd look at each pose and decide then if those with the hat were appropriate and tasteful.

When I viewed the photographer's samples and saw the one that is now my official headshot, I agreed to it immediately, and here's why. To me, the picture is nostalgic. Like a WWII-era photo of a wife posing on the pier with the cover of her just-returned sailor, The Hat Picture has a certain sweetness to it. It reminds me of the group photographs some Spouse Clubs take, dressed in their husbands' flight suits or uniforms, and send to the deployed squadron/unit/ship. It is an act similar to a high-school girl putting on her sweetheart's letter jacket or football jersey.

I'm Just Saying...

In fact, did you know that there is a tradition at the United States Naval Academy in which any girl who puts on a midshipmen's cover owes that man a kiss? This old-fashioned custom is actually printed in "Reef Points," a publication all midshipmen memorize during their Plebe Summer at the Academy.

The Hat Picture also brings to mind, or so I'm told, the moment when Debra Winger's character puts on the cover of flight student Zack Mayo (Richard Gere) in the movie "An Officer and a Gentleman."

While I understand some people's disapproval, I don't think most men object to a loved one donning their cover in that sweet, feminine way that Winger's character does.

My mom will be embarrassed for my saying this, but when I was growing up, she hung a poster on our kitchen door that read, "I love a man in uniform." Under the words was a picture of a very handsome, bare-chested male model posing in uniform pants with the jacket slung over his shoulder.

Some might say this was inappropriate and a misuse of the military uniform, but for my mom, the poster brought memories of her own man in uniform when he was away for so many months at a time. She didn't hang the poster to mimic or disgrace the uniform; she hung it because she really does love a man in a uniform!

One of the most appealing aspects of military life is the way it brings everyone, but especially couples, back to an old-fashioned, simpler way of living. For instance, my husband and I would probably not exchange letters if it weren't for his six-month deployments, when letters are our only contact. And while on most normal days I go to the base in my running pants and sweatshirt, on the day of homecoming, I always dress in heels and a nice skirt, following the long tradition of every woman who's ever greeted a returning sailor before me.

When I agreed to The Hat Picture, it was with these things in mind and was in no way meant to disgrace the uniform. I think it's obvious that I'm not trying to impersonate an officer. I'm simply displaying the feelings of pride so many military wives have for their husbands, the military...and the uniform. I was just following tradition. And yes, I did give my Naval Academy graduate a kiss after I wore the hat!

The Column You Never Saw

You checked today to see if I'm still wearing the hat, right?

I had an overwhelming amount of replies to this topic, and surprisingly (or not) only a handful of readers were against the hat. Countless people encouraged me to keep the hat. People even began yelling "Keep the hat!" to me from across grocery-store aisles and at the gas station. Military wives told me that they felt proud when they saw me, a fellow wife, wearing my husband's hat. Servicemen wrote to say they viewed the Hat Picture as a respectful tribute to the work they do.

Here's what some supporters said:

"Even though they are not on the payroll, Navy wives are a vital part of the Navy, so for you to pose in the hat seems perfectly appropriate to me."

"Keep the cover! To me you are honoring our service men and women."

"Keep the HAT as you are a member of the Smiley NAVY team. The act is a tradition and carries meaning."

"The angle you wear it at brings back plenty of memories. Down the gangplank after a cruise and during the first hugs somehow the sailor's hat usually ends up on his wife's head."

"[It] reminds us all that married to a sailor is married to the Navy."

"To me it shows your pride in your husband."

The few who are still upset about the hat, however, are vehemently against it. I take my reader's comments seriously, and in order not to trivialize the nay-sayers' feelings, I researched the legalities of the Hat Picture.

My wearing the hat is in fact against United States Code (10 USC, Subtitle A, Part II, Chapter 45, Sections 771 and 772). According to this, it is technically illegal for an unauthorized person to wear a military uniform or any recognizable piece of the uniform. The only exception: actors and actresses in a "theatrical setting" (a loop-hole giving men like Tom Cruise the right to wear a uniform in movies such as "Top Gun"). This code was created to prevent citizens from dressing up in uniform and impersonating an officer. It was also meant to keep anyone from associating themselves with the United States military (through the use of an official uniform) and defaming the service with degrading remarks or actions.

I was previously unaware of this code. Clearly. I think most people are. After 27 years of being a military dependent, I have always known that the uniform is something servicemen and women earn, and that it symbolizes respect, honor and commitment. I would never disregard this by wearing my husband's hat as if it were my own. In fact, I've never worn my husband's cover before or since this picture.

A reader wrote and asked, "It may be legal, but is it really right?" The reader felt that I was taking away the honor and respect service members earn with their uniform. This got me thinking, and I searched long and hard to understand my own intentions.

I strive to offer support and laughter to the spouses who wait at home, the ones on permanent shore duty. Being a military spouse is sometimes a lonely feeling. The worst is when a wife feels like she is the "only one." I want women to read my column and say, "Someone else feels this way, too!"

If wearing the hat in my picture draws these readers to my column so that I can offer them support, which in turn helps and supports their service-member counterparts, then my photo is doing a good thing.

To give up the Hat Picture for a handful of critics would be letting down the readers (both active duty and dependents) who wrote to tell me they are encouraged, proud, and full of patriotism when they see my photo.

My intention is to continue telling the military story, supporting those who wait at home, and paying tribute to those who serve. Apparently my photo is conveying this to a great majority of the readers. So until the U.S. military tells me otherwise, the hat stays put.

NOTE: Most readers never saw this column. It ran in one newspaper on a Tuesday, and shortly thereafter, I heard from the military. The Department of Defense, actually. I had to quickly write another, revised column (the one that follows) for the other newspapers that were about to publish this piece.

Six Months In Jail?
I Can Do That!

You checked today to see if I'm still wearing the hat, right? I had an overwhelming amount of replies to this topic, and surprisingly (or not) only a handful of readers were against the hat. Countless people wrote to encourage me to keep the hat and ignore the criticism. Military wives told me that they felt empowered and proud when they saw me, a fellow wife, wearing my husband's hat. Service men wrote to say that they viewed the "Hat Picture" as a respectful tribute to the work they do. One retired officer sent me photos of old recruiting posters from WWII featuring women in men's uniforms saying things like, "Gee, I wish I were a man and I'd join the U.S. Navy," and "If you want to fight, join the Marines." I'm sure you've seen these before—they are part of American history.

The few who are still upset about the hat, however, are vehemently against it. I take my reader's comments seriously, and in order not to trivialize the nay-sayers' feelings, I researched the legalities of "the Hat Picture."

My wearing the hat is in fact against the law (10 USC, Subtitle A, Part II, Chapter 45, Sections 771 and 772). According to this United States Code, it is illegal for a non-service member person to wear a military uniform or any recognizable piece of the uniform. The only exception is for actors and actresses in a "theatrical setting." This loop-hole was created to give men like Tom Cruise the right to wear a uniform in movies such as "Top Gun."

Wasn't my photo taken in a theatrical setting? It is a publicity photo for an entertainment column.

The answer is, no. Posing for a picture does not count as a "theatrical setting."

According to this law, all the military wives and children who have posed for a picture in their loved one's hat are breaking the law. Besides actual service men and women, only Hollywood has the right to wear a uniform.

What would my punishment be then, I wondered.

If charged, I could be fined $300 and sentenced to six months in prison.

Six months. I know a lot about six months. I've waited for six months while my husband was overseas supporting Operation Iraqi Freedom. I've watched my sons grow and change in the six months their dad was away. I've dealt with deaths and illnesses and setting up moves while I was alone for six months. How fitting then, that my punishment for wearing a military hat would be six months in jail.

But what about all the widowed military wives who turn their husband's pilot wings or uniform buttons into jewelry as a tribute to and remembrance of their departed loved one? Are these women breaking the law? Apparently they are. So should they be punished to six months in jail? Haven't they already suffered enough? Haven't they already served their six months over and over and over again?

This code was initially written to keep civilians from dressing up and impersonating an officer. I seriously doubt it was intended to keep wives from honoring their husbands—dead or alive. I got dozens of emails from servicemen saying that not only should it be legal for their wives to wear the hat for a picture, it should be their privilege. More than any other career, the military involves the commitment and sacrifice of the entire family. To say that wives are breaking the law by paying tribute to their husbands with an affectionate hat-wearing photo is to deny them the sacrifices they've made for the country as a military wife. Yes, my husband has worked very hard and earned his right to wear a military uniform, but am I so unimportant as a military wife that I could be thrown in jail for putting on his hat in a picture?

A reader wrote me and asked: Wearing the hat might be legal, but it is right?

I say, it may be illegal, but is it really wrong?

The Navy Wouldn't Want Me

My dad, a career Navy man of 32 years, is your typical service member—a straight-and-narrow, by-the-book, upstanding citizen. I don't think my dad's hair has ever touched his ears, and I'd be willing to bet my brand-new Nine West heels that he's never gotten a speeding ticket either.

With his strong connection to and fondness for the United States military, people often ask my dad, "Why didn't you send Sarah to the Naval Academy?"

And my dad says, "Because I wouldn't do that to the Navy."

Let's just say that waking up at 5 o'clock in the morning and taking quick showers isn't on my list of talents, and wearing my hair in any style other than that suggested by my trusted hairstylist sends waves of fear down my spine. I remember when I was a teenager my dad would say, "If sailors took showers as long as you do, there wouldn't be enough water on the ship."

Beyond my bathing and sleeping habits, however, the biggest reason I can't join the military is that I have a problem following the rules. I never read the directions on the back of the Trivial Pursuit box or any other game. This was a source of great conflict between my dad and me as I was growing up. Dad sees the world as black and white. I see it as many shades of Ralph Lauren gray.

A recent example of my against-the-rules behavior was, of course, the hat controversy (when I unknowingly broke a Federal code by wearing a military cover in my headshot), a situation which caused my dad to wipe his brow in relief that he is now retired and no longer claims me as a dependent, but also gave him further reason to believe I'd never make it as Ensign Sarah Smiley.

Sometimes, I guess, when I believe in something, I have a hard time letting it go. This type of rebellious attitude doesn't mesh well with the military, and I'd probably have a hard time accepting all of the Navy's rules. When the Navy told my dad "Go," he went, even if it was Christmas or his daughter was about to be born. I, on the other hand, have a hard enough time leaving my game of Chutes and Ladders with my son to go wash the dishes.

Now I'm married to another straight-and-narrow Navy man. Dustin sympathizes with my dad as he is now the one who enters the house with caution, wondering what I'm up to and what trouble I've caused. He usually takes this in stride and actually loves (or claims to, at least) my spontaneous nature that is so unlike his own. But recently, when Dustin and I were having a discussion, he got stubborn with me. "Sarah," he said, "this is America and you have many freedoms, but freedom is not without cost, and you simply can't go around doing whatever you please."

Gee, I feel as if I've heard this before, I thought. Oh yes, it was from my dad!

Just between you and me though, Dustin and Dad are right. We don't have the freedom to speed when we're driving (although many do it anyway), to jaywalk or to run a red light. There are some laws, no matter how trivial they seem, which are put in place for the common good, and it isn't our freedom to disregard them.

The rules and regulations placed on members of the military are lengthy and demanding, but the noble men and women of the armed forces accept and follow them in a selfless, heroic way. Dustin follows the Navy's standards for his haircut, his uniform and his behavior without ever complaining. I watch in amazement as he measures the distance between each medal on his uniform, making sure it is correct. He is so exact, always by the book ... just like someone else I know. And he does it all to be part of something bigger and greater than himself.

Not everyone is cut out for this rigorous way of being, and those who do it every day should be commended. The men and women of the military have given up many of their own personal freedoms in order to protect ours. It is a sacrifice many of us can't imagine or comprehend, but one that should always be respected.

Yes, it's true, I'm not made for the military, and I couldn't fill a service member's shoes. Alright, so I can't fill their hat either. I simply don't have it in me. So you can rest tonight, Mom—I won't be enlisting anytime soon. Because honestly folks, Dad was right. The Navy probably wouldn't want me.

I'm Just Saying...

Acknowledgements

This book began after several cocktails at a release party for a bridal magazine in Pensacola, Fla. I ran into Malcolm Ballinger, my publisher at *Pensacola Magazine*, and said on a whim, "Say, would you consider publishing a book of my columns?"

Malcolm, who reminds me of Robert De Niro (but not in a creepy "Cape Fear" sort of way), scratched his chin and said in that wonderful English accent of his, "Yes, I would. What do you have in mind?"

A few months later, Dustin and I met Malcolm and his wife, Glenys, for dinner at the Global Grill in downtown Pensacola. A book was born. All of which is to say, without Malcolm, you would not be holding this book in your hands right now. Thank you, Malcolm and Glenys.

There were, of course, plenty of other people who helped me along the way, and I will try to mention all of them now.

Kelly Oden, my editor at Ballinger Publishing, has been an indispensable wealth of ideas, information and support because ... well, because she "gets it." Thank you for always being just a phone call or email away.

My newspaper column might never have been syndicated without the patient, yet enthusiastic, advice and support of James McCarthy at *The Times-Record* in Brunswick, Maine. Other editors who have helped and encouraged me along the way are Miriam Gallett, *JaxAirNews*; Joan Krauter, *The Bradenton Herald*; and Carl Surran, *Military Money*.

I owe an enormous thanks to Carol Leifer and Ward Carroll for their forewords, but also for their friendship and support.

Thank you to my mom and dad, Van and Kelly, Will and Cindy,

my in-laws Robin and Phil, and Megan (who is mentioned in "I Think I Learned Too Much This Summer" as being "childless," but now is the mother of baby Lyla) and Brett.

Thank you, as always, to Tracy Bernstein, Jenny Bent and Shari Smiley.

Thank you to St. Luke UMC, Dr. F., Kevin and Linda Berry, the Pearces, the Adams, Larry and Mary Lou Garrett (who read my column every single week), the families of HT-18, Heidi Kennedy (she saved me from insanity), John and Margaret Andrade, Darcy and Kristi.

Last, I would be totally remiss if I did not mention the true stars of my column, my four boys: Dustin, Ford, Owen and Lindell. Thank you, Dustin, for allowing me to write about your not-so-finer moments, but mostly, for having a great sense of humor.

Ford, Owen and Lindell: everything I've done has always been, and will continue to be, for you. Thank you for your funny comments and unique perspective on the world. I hope this book serves as a record of your childhood that you will cherish and someday share with your own family. I love you all. And not just because I'm your mother.

About
Sarah Smiley

Navy wife Sarah Smiley is the author of "Shore Duty," a syndicated newspaper column that reaches more than two million readers weekly, and the memoir *Going Overboard: The Misadventures of a Military Wife* (Penguin/New American Library, 2005).

Sarah has been featured in *The New York Times Magazine* ("Confessions of a Military Wife," November 6, 2005) and *Newsweek*, and on ABC's "Nightline," CNN "American Morning," CNN "Sunday Morning," CBS "The Early Show," Fox News "Studio B," and MSNBC "Live."

Film and dramatic rights are represented by Shari Smiley (surprisingly, no relation) at Creative Artist Agency in Los Angeles, Calif. Sarah's literary work is represented by Jenny Bent at Trident Media Group in New York.

Sarah has been a Navy dependent for more than 31 years. She is the daughter of Lindell Rutherford, a career Navy F-14 pilot, and spent most of her upbringing amid the aircraft carriers and Navy bases in Virginia Beach, Va.

Sarah Smiley has a B.S. in Education from Samford University in Birmingham, Ala. She is the mother of three young boys—Ford (7), Owen (5), and baby Lindell (1)—and the wife of a Navy pilot, Lt. Cmdr. Dustin Smiley.

Read more about Sarah at www.sarahsmiley.com.

About Carol Leifer

Hailed by *Washington Post* as "refreshing" and "one of the best comedic minds of our time," Carol Leifer is an acclaimed stand-up comedian and Emmy-nominated writer.

Carol is working on her first book for Random House, entitled *When You Lie About Your Age, The Terrorists Win*. She is also touring the country with a one-woman show of the same name.

Carol, a Long Island native, began her career as a comic in such well-known clubs as The Comic Strip, Catch A Rising Star and The Improv. An unexpected visit from David Letterman to The Comic Strip led to twenty-five appearances on NBC's "Late Night With David Letterman" and the production of Carol's Cinemax special called "Carol Doesn't Leifer Anymore."

Shortly thereafter, Carol wrote, produced and starred in three specials for Showtime: "Carol Leifer Comedy Cruise," "Really Big Shoo," and "Gaudy, Bawdy, and Blue," which was nominated for three cable ACE Awards. She also appeared in HBO's "Young Comedians Special" and the Rodney Dangerfield Special: "Nothin' Goes Right." Leifer also starred in her own stand-up special for Comedy Central.

One of Carol's greatest career dreams came true when she appeared with Johnny Carson on "The Tonight Show" two months prior to his retirement.

Carol's writing career began when she became a staff writer for the seminal comedy show "Saturday Night Live." She moved on to writing sitcoms, joining the staff of "Seinfeld," where she contributed to over seventy-five episodes, eventually becoming a producer of the show. Following that, Carol served as writer and supervising producer on HBO's critically-acclaimed "The Larry Sanders Show." Leifer then went on to become executive producer and co-creator of "The Ellen Show" on CBS. Carol worked as writer and co-executive producer for the 2007-2008 season of the CBS hit show "Rules of Engagement." Carol is also a regular writer for the Academy Awards.

About Ward Carroll

Ward Carroll is the editor of Military.com, responsible for all news, editorials, commentaries and other content on the site and in newsletters.

During his 20-year Navy career, Ward served in four different F-14 squadrons and accumulated more than 2,800 flight hours in operations that included five extended aircraft carrier deployments to hostile regions. His last tour on active duty was at his alma mater, the U.S. Naval Academy, where he taught English, leadership, and ethics. He retired at the rank of commander. Immediately following his retirement, he worked as the communications director for the V-22 Osprey program at the Naval Air Systems Command.

Ward's writing has appeared in a wide variety of periodicals, including *Golf World*, *Hits*, and *Proceedings*. He was editor of *Approach* magazine as a lieutenant and is currently a contributing editor for *Naval Aviation News*. His three novels about a Tomcat pilot—*Punk's War* (2001), *Punk's Wing* (2003), and *Punk's Fight* (2004)—have been widely praised for their realistic portrayals of a Naval Aviator's life. He earned the Naval Institute Press' "Author of the Year" honors in 2001. He has two other published works: *The Aide* (2005) and *Militia Kill* (2006). He currently blogs at Defensetech.org, and at his personal site, wardcarroll.com.

Ward's military decorations include the Strike Flight Air Medal, the Meritorious Service Medal, and the Navy/Marine Corps Commendation Medal (four awards). He is married with two teenaged sons and splits his time between southern Maryland and San Francisco.